The Defenses of Northern New Spain

Number Four: DeGolyer Library Series

THE DEFENSES OF

Southern Methodist University Press

NORTHERN NEW SPAIN

Hugo O'Conor's Report to Teodoro de Croix, July 22, 1777

Edited and Translated by Donald C. Cutter

DeGolyer Library · Dallas · 1994

First edition, 1994

Requests for permission to reproduce material from
this work should be sent to:

Permissions
Southern Methodist University Press
Box 415, Dallas, Texas 75275

Library of Congress Cataloging-in-Publication Data

Oconor, Hugo.
     The defenses of northern New Spain : Hugo O'Conor's report
to Teodoro de Croix, July 22, 1977 / edited and translated by
Donald C. Cutter. – 1st ed.
          p.   cm. – (De Golyer Library Series ; no. 1)
     Includes index.
     ISBN 0-87074-347-3
     1. Southwest, New – History – to 1848.   2. Southwest, New – Defenses.
3. New Spain – Defenses.   4. Apache Indians – Wars.   I. Cutter, Donald C.
II. Title.   III. Series.
F799.033 1994
979'.01 – dc20   93-18212

*The Summerlee Foundation in Dallas, Texas
provided assistance for the production of this book.*

DESIGNED AND PRINTED BY W. THOMAS TAYLOR
TITLE PAGE DRAWING BY JOSÉ CISNEROS

Contents

Foreword

In Mexico City in May 1777, a cranky Lieutenant Colonel Hugo O'Conor penned a lengthy report to his successor, Teodoro de Croix, explaining how to defend New Spain's vast northern provinces from further Apache assaults. O'Conor knew whereof he spoke. For the last dozen years, since his arrival in New Spain in 1765, he had served continuously on the viceroyalty's northern frontier. His assignments had included stints as a garrison commander, as acting governor of Texas, and as inspector in chief of Spanish military forces. In the latter post he supervised garrisons throughout New Spain's *provincias internas*, or internal provinces, as contemporaries knew northern New Spain. In present-day terms, his jurisdiction embraced the southwestern states of California, New Mexico, Arizona, and Texas, and the northern tier of Mexican states—Baja California, Sonora, Sinaloa, Chihuahua (then part of Nueva Vizcaya), and Coahuila.

As O'Conor's replacement in 1777, Teodoro de Croix faced a daunting task in curtailing Indian raiders over such a vast expanse, but O'Conor assured his successor that his difficulties paled in comparison to those that O'Conor had confronted when he assumed command of the interior provinces in 1771. Then, O'Conor explained, Apaches wreaked havoc across the frontier, and especially in Nueva Vizcaya. O'Conor, however, convened a military council in April 1772 that mapped out a strategy. O'Conor implemented this strategy by increasing patrols, relocating fortifications, reforming the military supply system, and personally leading military campaigns against the Apaches. "I fortunately came out victorious," O'Conor noted, "reestablishing the honor of the King's arms."

Step by step, O'Conor went on to instruct his novice successor in techniques for continuing the war against the Apaches: how to synchronize patrols, how to coordinate a large-scale offensive campaign, and what tactics and routes to employ. O'Conor concluded with praise for the fighting skills of the Hispanic frontiersmen, and with thumbnail sketches of Indian peoples across the frontier, from Yaquis and Pimas in the west to Comanches and Karankawas in the east.

The DeGolyer Library is pleased to make O'Conor's valuable report more readily accessible and is grateful to the Summerlee Foundation for support of this publication. It is published here for the first time in English, and for the first time in its entirety in Spanish. O'Conor's report has appeared in print only once before, as a small book published in Mexico City in 1952. But the editors of that edition worked from an incomplete copy of O'Conor's original manuscript. They lacked the final two paragraphs of his report, hindering them from identifying Croix as the recipient of the report or giving it a precise date. And they worked from a manuscript that apparently lacked the three tables that accompanied O'Conor's report. The present edition is based on a complete contemporary copy of the manuscript once owned by Dr. Nicolás León, and now in the DeGolyer Library. Everett Lee DeGolyer, Jr. purchased the manuscript in 1968, from H. P. Kraus, for his private library. When that library went to Southern Methodist University in 1973, O'Conor's manuscript was among its many treasures.

We are also pleased that Donald C. Cutter graciously agreed to translate and edit the O'Conor report, and to write an introduction that places it and its author in the context of the times. The dean of Borderlands historians and the former president of both the Western History Association and the Pacific Coast Branch of the American Historical Association, Donald Cutter trained much of the present generation of scholars of the early Hispanic Southwest. Cutter earned his Ph.D. at the University of California, Berkeley, studying under such luminaries as Herbert Eugene Bolton, Lawrence Kinnaird, and George P. Hammond. After receiving his doctorate, Cutter went on to train his own disciples, numbering some forty-six Ph.D.s, primarily during his long tenure at the University of Southern California and the University of New Mexico. He ended his active teaching career at St. Mary's University in San Antonio, where he held the O'Connor Chair of Spanish Colonial History of Texas and the Southwest. Since his retirement in December 1987, he has continued to divide his time between his homes in Madrid and Albuquerque, and to contribute vigorously to greater understanding of Spanish activity in North America through public lectures, writing, and consulting for museums and television. His best-known works treat Spanish maritime exploration along the California coast and the Pacific Northwest, with books such as *Malaspina in Cal-*

ifornia (1960), *The California Coast: A Bilingual Edition of Documents* (1969), and three recent titles, *California in 1792: A Spanish Naval Visit* (1990), *Malaspina and Galiano: Spanish Voyages to the Northwest Coast, 1791-1792* (1991), and *España en Nuevo México* (1992). Those publications assure his scholarly reputation, while his warmth, wisdom, and generosity of spirit have won him the enduring affection and gratitude of a generation of graduate students.

David Farmer
Associate Director, Central University Libraries
and Head, DeGolyer Library

David J. Weber
Dedman Professor of History
Southern Methodist University

Introduction

In 1764 Hugo O'Conor, a ruddy thirty-year-old Irishman, landed at Veracruz, the major eastern seaport of colonial Mexico. It was the initial mainland step of a man who rapidly became a leading Spanish officer on the northern frontier of New Spain. In the decade and a half that followed his arrival, he made his mark on the Spanish Southwest in no uncertain terms. His apparent importance has been enhanced by the curiosity of his name, for clearly Hugo O'Conor, even when spelled the Spanish way,[1] has the advantage of easy recognition by non-Hispanic scholars amid the hundreds of contemporary more obviously Spanish names. I must confess to being initially attracted to O'Conor through his name, which I mentally archived along with that of Alejandro O'Reilly and other prominent late colonial figures of apparently similar background such as Juan O'Donojú and Bernardo O'Higgins.

1. J. Ignacio Rubio Mañé, "El Teniente Coronel don Hugo O'Conor y la situación en Chihuahua, año de 1771," *Boletín del Archivo General de la Nación*, vol. 30, no. 3, p. 359, points out that in documentation existing in that repository Hugo always signed his name O'Conor, not O'Connor.

The nearly fifteen years that O'Conor of Ireland, a Dublin-born Catholic and a political nonconformist, spent on the northern frontier of New Spain coincided, not entirely accidentally, with a period of vigorous pursuit of a new, somewhat visionary Spanish policy in relation to its outermost northern defensive perimeter. O'Conor was initially sent to report on one segment of the irregular defense line, but ended up in charge of implementing a grand plan to pacify and secure all of that distant frontier. For reasons more connected to events elsewhere, O'Conor's successes and failures came and went. Lack of complete support, internal problems, external threats, and personality conflicts conditioned his active years in what is today the Spanish Southwest of the United States and the northern states of Mexico.

In addition to his military participation in frontier planning and field operations, O'Conor was a good recorder of events, a factor that makes him much more accessible to brief biographical treatment. To attract a biographer, a historical figure almost invariably must have written copiously, regularly, and cogently. A second factor is having been an observer or participant in important events. Hugo O'Conor fits into both categories, but as yet has not become the subject of a full-scale biography.

The best published source for information concerning his life and activities is J[orge] Ignacio Rubio Mañé in his "Nota Introductoria" of "El Teniente Coronel Don Hugo O'Conor y la situación en Chihuahua, año de 1771," which is followed by an "Itinerario del Teniente Coronel Don Hugo O'Conor, de la Ciudad de México a la villa de Chihuahua, 1771."[2] A good summary of O'Conor's life also appears in David M. Vigness, "Don Hugo Oconor and New Spain's Northeastern Frontier, 1764–1776."[3] A third summary is contained in Luis Navarro García, *Don José de Gálvez y la Comandancia General de las Provincias Internas del Norte de Nueva España.*[4]

There are few figures who are more familiar in Borderlands history than Don Hugo. The intrusiveness of his name in the documentation of the second half of the eighteenth century must be one of the reasons that he is well known, for an Irish name was a rarity on the northern frontier. A certain amount of non-Hispanic ethnocentrism is evident in a person's first contact with the one-time commandant inspector, and it is carried over to courses in History of the Spanish Southwest in which the Irish officer's name inevitably appears as an identification question on the typical midterm or final examination. It could be argued that the examiner, desiring to break the monotony of Hispanic name after name, puts O'Conor in the list, with little or no regard for his importance. But such an explanation is not very logical in view of his importance to the story of a large part of the Borderlands during a brief period when he was the most important person there. For O'Conor plays a role in the history of Texas, New Mexico, and Arizona, and an even larger role in the story of the north Mexican states of Sonora, Chihuahua, and Coahuila.

Was he well known in his own time? The answer is yes. He was highly regarded by several viceroys, particularly Antonio María Bucareli, and seemingly well known to such leading figures as Visitor General José de Gálvez, Bernardo de Gálvez, and Teodoro de Croix. While in Texas, O'Conor had met the Marqués de Rubí, who was there on his famous and important inspection from which evolved the line of presidios that O'Conor was later ordered to reform, implement, and deal with as senior military commander in the area. He was also very well known to another important frontier figure, Alejandro O'Reilly. In fact, O'Conor's presence in the New World and in the Spanish army was in large measure

2. These contributions by Rubio Mañé are found in *Boletín del Archivo General de la Nación*, vol. 30, pp. 355–91, and in the same volume of the *Boletín*, pp. 395–471 and 647–55.

3. The study by David Vigness first appeared in *Journal of the West*, vol. 6, (January 1967), pp. 28–35. It was later reprinted in Oakah L. Jones, Jr., *The Spanish Borderlands: A First Reader* (Los Angeles, 1974), pp. 170–83.

4. Published Sevilla, 1964; see pp. 331–44.

owing to Don Alejandro, his elder cousin in whose footsteps he walked. In a day when nepotism was well established, and particularly so in Spain, having a highly placed relative who also served as patron was not infrequent. The oft-heard refrain *quien no tiene padrino, no tiene bautizo* (he who doesn't have a godfather doesn't get baptized), is not restricted to the baptismal font. Kinsman and fellow Irish mercenary O'Reilly paved the way for some of Hugo O'Conor's successes. This is not to infer that the younger cousin was incompetent, but rather that patronage placed him in the enviable position of being favored over persons of equivalent merit.

O'Conor was not only known in the higher circles of Spanish colonial bureaucracy, he was also known on the more intimate level of the areas where he served. Clearly not a run-of-the-mill person, he seems to have been both charismatic and outgoing. When in Texas, early in his career in the Borderlands, he was referred to as "El Capitán Colorado." This has led some historians who have subjected him to brief biographical treatment to think that he was so called because he was a redhead in an area where blond was rare, brown fairly common, and black the most frequent hair pigment. But the word for redhead is normally *pelirrojo*. In the context of the mid-eighteenth century, it is more likely that *colorado* meant florid or ruddy, and referred to his general appearance and not to the color of his hair (which might have been red or not).[5]

O'Conor was born in the capital of Ireland in December 1734 and was baptized on the day before Christmas, the second child of Daniel O'Connor, a native of Roscommon in Connaught province, and of Margarita O'Ryan, who was a native of Dublin. The family had for some time distinguished itself in the almost continual uprisings of the Irish populace against British control. It is even indicated that the O'Connor family was descended from the last king of Connaught who had lost his throne in 1224. Hugo's father and grandfather were revolutionaries. His grandfather had fled to Spain in 1652 and remained there until the restoration of the monarchy under Charles II in 1660. Being of such antecedents, and having participated unsuccessfully in rebellion, it is not surprising that young Hugo expatriated himself in about 1751 to Spain, following the lead of two of his cousins of the O'Reilly family who had found a warm reception in a coreligionist, anti-British stronghold. In Spain such rebels were well received as political and religious refugees. As Vigness put it, O'Conor "was one of the 'Wild Geese' of Ire-

5. Navarro García in his *José de Gálvez*, pp. 198–99, also expresses the opinion that the nickname "Capitán Colorado" derived from O'Connor's ruddy face.

land who, having lost their birthrights or prejudiced their freedom in conflict with Protestant England, sought a haven in other lands." The destination of many such refugees was either in Catholic France or Spain.[6]

Already possessed of practical military experience, O'Conor rose from cadet in 1751 to lieutenant in the Infantry Regiment of Hibernia.[7] In 1762 he was promoted to captain and first adjutant major of a new Regiment of Volunteers of Aragón, possibly through the intervention of one or the other of his cousins, either Spanish Field Marshal Don Alejandro O'Reilly or Colonel Don Domingo O'Reilly, who was at that time a *gentilhombre de manga*, a sort of tutor-protector of the Infante Don Antonio Pascual, twelfth child of King Carlos II and Queen María Amalia.

Following rapid recruitment of his new regiment in Zaragoza, Lieutenant O'Conor and his group went off to the Portuguese Wars. His unit took part in the vanguard of the campaign there, participating in the siege of Almeida and the capture of Chaves, Miranda, and other places in the north. O'Conor's next activity was in the New World. As Mexican scholar Rubio Mañé points out, from the year 1763 forward there was a great military movement of personnel from Spain to America, with deployment of as many troops as possible under veteran officers who had been seasoned in the long recent campaigns in Italy where Spain had been defending its interests. The great trans-Atlantic movement of troops had as its primary goal Cuba and subsequently New Spain, areas continually threatened by British naval forces. The purpose was that of mounting an improved defense of those overseas possessions and attempting to retake the insular capital of Havana, which had fallen into enemy hands as a result of an early British success in the Seven Years' War. O'Conor was named as sergeant major of the high command of the new governor, the Conde de Ricla. At the time of his displacement to Cuba, Don Hugo had already reached that advanced military rank. In that same year of 1763, as a measure of his level of progress and future promise, he was made a knight of the prestigious Order of Calatrava, a distinction that most contemporary military men avidly sought.

O'Conor served in Cuba for about two years under the general command of Field Marshal O'Reilly, his cousin, who had been in charge of the military renovation of that island's defenses. Don Hugo's assignment involved mostly the training of militia forces. In early March of

6. Vigness, "Don Hugo Oconor, 1764–1776," p. 172.

7. Though O'Conor's service in large measure involved essentially cavalry operations with mounted troops such as the buckskin-clad dragoons, and with the rapid deployment forces or *compañías volantes*, he was always an infantry officer.

1765, Sergeant Major O'Conor went off in the vessel *El Aquiles* to Veracruz with some other officers of equal rank, forming part of a group sent to reinforce that coastal city. They were part of the forces sent with other officers to Veracruz accompanying Don Juan de Villalba, a senior officer who had been ordered to reorganize the army of New Spain. In his new assignment O'Conor's service branch designation was general staff, detached (*estado mayor suelto*).

Soon after his arrival O'Conor was ordered to Mexico City by the Viceroy Marqués de Cruillas. His new mainland assignment was as commanding officer of the Legión del Príncipe, which was doing garrison duty in the city of Guanajuato. While serving there O'Conor received an official letter from Minister of the Indies Julián de Arriaga written from the Palace at El Pardo, near Madrid. It was in response to an earlier request that O'Conor had made for promotion to lieutenant colonel and command of the then vacant northern presidio of San Sabá, open as a result of the death of its commanding officer Felipe Rábago y Terán. The letter was a positive response granting O'Conor the desired promotion and command, provided there had not been any change in the future plans for that establishment in central Texas. It was a move not soon implemented.

The viceroy was impressed by O'Conor and resolved initially to send the Irishman out with more important business than command of a frontier post such as San Sabá. Instead, the viceroy selected him to proceed to Texas to perform in that troubled area certain "urgent duties," which called for him to operate with prudence and moderation.

In the fall of 1765, O'Conor and a comrade, Lieutenant Melchor Afán de Rivera, went first to San Agustín de Ahumada Presidio on the lower Trinity River. There the Irish newcomer arrested the acting commanding officer, Marcos Ruíz, on charges of having abused his authority in matters involving presidial supply. Furthermore, both Ruíz and his men had been involved in damages to the local presidio resulting from a skirmish with other provincial troops. Lieutenant Afán de Rivera was placed in temporary command of the Presidio de San Agustín de Ahumada, while the prisoners taken by O'Conor were turned over to the governor of Texas, Angel Martos y Navarrete.

More important was O'Conor's business with Martos. The viceroy wanted O'Conor to investigate the events that stemmed from bitter hostility between Governor Martos of Texas and the captain of the presidio at Orcoquisac, Rafael Martínez Pacheco. The enmity between the two had culminated in the burning of the Orcoquisac fortification. The charges involved not only the governor of Texas but also a group of his men. There was the added report that Martos had apparently solicited a willing participant for the assassination of his rival.

O'Conor quickly put things in their true light. Among the allegations was that the governor was the key man in smuggling operations taking place in Texas. Contraband trade was certainly not unknown, but there were strict orders to prohibit commerce with foreigners and strong evidence that Martos was not observing such laws. On 9 June 1767 O'Conor was able to submit his detailed report to the viceroy, who by that time was the Marqués de Croix. As a consequence of such information, on 14 July Martos was recalled and required to present himself to answer charges before Croix within no less than one month. Most of the accusations against Martos were gleaned from O'Conor's report, written as early as 27 March. Martos's departure left the Irishman as senior officer present in the colony, and in July 1767 O'Conor received orders to impound all goods that belonged to the governor both in Los Adaes and San Antonio, the two principal Texas settlements.

On 28 August 1767, O'Conor became governor *ad interim*. He was serving in that capacity when the Marqués de Rubí made a well-known Borderlands inspection as a preliminary to a general realignment of the frontier military defenses and institution of an integrated Indian policy. Rubí found in O'Conor a willing subordinate and colleague, one who agreed with and had a close appreciation of the changes that Rubí would soon propose for the area of Texas. In this regard O'Conor was of the opinion that the traditional provincial capital of Los Adaes was useless as a presidial post, a judgment that was identical to that of the inspector, and perhaps originated with him, finding easy acceptance by the Irishman in his role as host to Rubí's visitation.

While acting governor, O'Conor reaped an amount of local criticism as a result of his strict enforcement of existing, but often unheeded, provisions against trading with foreigners, which had been conveniently overlooked by his predecessor. Navarro García credits O'Conor with carrying out well his duties, and doing as much as possible to maintain friendly relations with the Indians. It should be pointed out that this "cordiality" followed a three-hour-long battle on 7 December 1767 that O'Conor waged against local Indians on the banks of the Guadalupe River in central Texas. The odds had been against victory, as the twenty Spanish troops were outnumbered by three hundred natives; but the death of twenty Indians resulted in at least a temporary increase of respect for Spanish arms.

According to Vigness, O'Conor also welcomed the challenge presented by the need to deal with the more warlike Indians of the western area of Texas. To implement his strategy, he moved his headquarters from Los Adaes to San Antonio de Béxar, thereby shifting the seat of government permanently toward the southwest. On the basis of what must have been a successful series of campaigns, and feeling that his mission in Texas had been accomplished, O'Conor was prompted to ask for a leave of absence. This did not materialize for another year, until in early 1770 he was relieved of the governorship by the Barón de Ripperdá. O'Conor returned to Mexico City with full approval by the viceroy of the "high efficiency with which he had discharged his duty."[8]

8.Vigness, "Don Hugo Oconor," p. 178.

By May 1770, O'Conor was back in Mexico City, since at that date he was a witness in the case of Martos, the ex-governor of Texas. O'Conor's earlier request for promotion to lieutenant colonel with command of San Sabá Presidio was still pending. He was still on the books as commandant of the Legión del Príncipe stationed at Guanajuato. It is probable that a recommendation by O'Reilly improved O'Conor's chances, and he was soon named to the presidial command of San Sabá. Founded in 1757 near what is today Menard, Texas, the presidio had been moved below the Rio Grande to San Fernando de Austria, at what is now Zaragoza, Coahuila.

After appointment to San Sabá, there is indication that O'Conor went into the northern areas and campaigned against the Indians. However, in late summer 1771 he was once more in Mexico City where he was assigned by Marqués de Croix to a position placing him in charge of the frontier. As Croix was soon to be replaced by Bucareli, O'Conor waited in the capital until Bucareli arrived so as to have opportunity to meet with the newly appointed viceroy.

The Viceroy Marqués de Croix had already determined to send the Irishman in a new role that had been contemplated for quite some time. On 9 September 1771, the viceroy wrote to O'Conor indicating that he had named him Commandant Inspector of the Internal Presidios for the purpose of putting into practice the new instructions and regulations for the better establishment and governance of those presidios, with a salary of four thousand pesos a year. "In consequence of which I hope that you will accept the mentioned appointment and you will dedicate your time to carrying out that duty with the same effort and prudence that I confidently expect from your proven zeal and love of the service, as well as all the appropriate assets that you possess."[9]

The new post came as a direct result of the earlier mentioned Rubí inspection, which had been followed by several deliberative juntas. In his new position Hugo O'Conor was made not only commandant inspector of the troops of the leading northern province of Chihuahua, but also of the rest of the frontier. In the operation plan, five presidios were to be moved. In order to implement the new project, O'Conor's request was authorized for enlargement of the Chihuahua garrison and for an additional four rapid deployment companies. Some historians have referred to these as the "flying companies."

Much information concerning O'Conor's tenure as commandant inspector comes from a letter directed to his successor, Teodoro de Croix, nephew of the viceroy whom O'Conor served with full satisfaction. From it we learn of the successes and some of the failures of the five years that O'Conor served in his new role.

Besides information contained in the Irishman's reports, what do we know of the life of the author, a man who by that time was middle-aged? First, we can assume that he had a good education as judged by his logical presentation of material and his command of Spanish, which was not his native language. In fact, though we are working from a contemporary copy, it displays complete control of his adopted language. It is always possible that some errors stemming from his alien background might have been combed out by a scribe in composing this copy, but there is no special reason to believe it to be so. Second, we can assume that he was a fit and able soldier, based on his quick rise in the officer ranks and on the confidence reposed in him by various persons whose reports are extant. Third, we can see that he did not have the complete backing of some people, nor did he view some of his colleagues with great enthusiasm. However, he had considerable support from Bucareli, which, although it has not been specifically ascribed to such a connection, was without doubt enhanced by a strong personal friendship between Bucareli and Alejandro O'Reilly. This closeness dated from at least as early as the period that Bucareli spent as governor and captain general of Cuba and Field Marshal O'Reilly, O'Conor's cousin, served the captaincy general of Cuba in restructuring its defenses and in the successful conquest of Louisiana.

The first several paragraphs of O'Conor's report, in the form of an extremely lengthy letter written to the man who was in essence taking over his duties as senior commander of the northern frontier, evoke sym-

9. Marqués de Croix to Hugo O'Conor, Mexico, 9 September 1771, from the Archivo General de la Nación and printed in Rubio Mañé, "El Teniente Coronel Don Hugo O'Conor," p. 360.

pathy. O'Conor cannot mask obvious feelings that his successor was paying no attention whatsoever to the work that had been carried out by O'Conor. He complains about his measures having been set aside, and that the new commander-in-chief was not availing himself of the advantage of prior reports. The Irishman was greatly displeased by Teodoro de Croix's lack of interest in past experience, particularly in view of the fact that as far as the frontier was concerned Don Teodoro was a tenderfoot and O'Conor was a hardened veteran of four major and difficult campaigns of Indian pacification and over a decade of service in the area.

There is also the possibility that in the long report O'Conor was doing his utmost to justify his period of incumbency, portraying his efforts in the brightest hues possible. This is accompanied by the not unusual stance in the same report of indicating how bad things were when he took command of the area succeeding Bernardo de Gálvez. In this painting of a bleak picture of things in 1771, it was necessary for O'Conor to walk circumspectly, which he did. Bernardo de Gálvez was probably miscast as a frontier commander, and had not been notably successful. But his uncle, Visitor General José de Gálvez, had just been recalled to Spain, where he was soon to be elevated to Minister of the Indies and given the title Marqués de Sonora. Don José wanted his nephew Bernardo to accompany him back to Spain and to that end the frontier commander had been replaced by Hugo O'Conor. It was not in O'Conor's self-interest to be too critical of his predecessor, and yet he had to establish a dismal picture of frontier conditions in order to make his accomplishments stand out in brilliant relief. To do this, he played up the bravery of Don Bernardo, who had carried out some offensive operations and had been wounded in battle by the local Indians, and O'Conor used this as an explanation for the unsuccessful performance of José de Gálvez's nephew. It was a hard and potentially dangerous course that O'Conor had to steer, but he emerged unscathed. By the time of the writing of his report, he had the confidence of the now long-departed uncle and apparently no difficulty with his own predecessor, Bernardo. Had O'Conor been more specific, he probably would have lost the good will of both of those men. In the more critical words of Viceroy Bucareli, slowness of the change of command from Bernardo de Gálvez to O'Conor had been because "the *Visitador's* nephew had gone out with many hopes of quieting the Indians, and returned with [nothing but] a wound."[10]

In O'Conor's report, he leaves the impression that by dint of his great

10. Letter of Bucareli to Alejandro O'Reilly as quoted in Bernard E. Bobb, *The Viceregency of Antonio María Bucareli in New Spain, 1771–1779* (Austin, 1962), p. 131.

efforts, coupled with the support of both the bureaucracy and his local troops, his era was one that brought peace to the frontier. There is no doubt that his time of service there saw many important events, and in some measure he was responsible for the results that made this period as important as it was. His tenure coincided with an era of maximum effort to promote the security of the frontier. In this regard, it was a transition period from local efforts at defense as circumstances dictated to a coordinated plan for security of the entire frontier from Arizona eastward to Texas. It was a magnificent plan, one destined to have less success once implemented than it appeared to have on the planning board. But Hugo O'Conor was in on the initial implementation of the line of presidios, and died long before it was fully evident that it was not the cure-all that it had seemed to promise.

O'Conor's period in control of the frontier was one of ceaseless military campaigns along the newly arranged line, one in which there was cooperation between presidios, one in which Indian auxiliaries took active part, and one that used the mobile companies of the frontier, the rapid deployment forces, as troubleshooting units to be transferred as exigencies required. In an effort for maximum success, O'Conor was involved in an increasingly widespread Indian policy in which new alliances were made by Spain with native groups that had not previously been in the Spanish camp. It is not to be expected that O'Conor would have viewed with any modern sense of morality the problem of control of regional Indians. He was a product of his time and of its thinking. This was Spain's land; the Indians were subjects of his sovereign; and they owed allegiance to Carlos III. The Irish expatriate did not think in terms of the inherent right of aboriginal occupancy and possession, nor can we expect him to have done so. His job as a senior military officer assigned to implement a new defensive scheme for the northernmost portion of a far-flung colonial empire was to insure its security both in the present and in the foreseeable future. Furthermore, he was expected to do the best with what he had, or what by means of his frequent reports to Viceroy Bucareli he was able to get from a colonial administration perennially short on funds and always trying to economize. O'Conor personally felt obliged to be continually engaged in implementation of the plan of presidios and in military campaigns against Indians thought to be enemies. In this regard, that of personal field participation, O'Conor was far more active than his successor, Teodoro de Croix, who on his part was very critical of O'Conor. Historian Alfred Barnaby Thomas, who has studied the career of Teodoro de Croix, feels that during O'Conor's regime "nothing was done to alleviate any fundamental difficulties."[11]

Even though O'Conor had no direct connection with the major frontier expansion into the new area of Upper California that was taking place, the troops under his general control were involved in seeking a trail to transport colonists from the relatively settled area of Sonora to the hinterland of what one day would become the Golden State. It was expansion beyond the scope of the Rubí plan and caused it to have some unforeseen weaknesses. Certainly any ideas of expansion of the frontier were beyond the imagination of O'Conor, whose time and energy were consumed by the constant urgency of holding off the Apache invasion of existing settlements. If, as Navarro García says, there was any thought on O'Conor's part of advancing the location of any presidios, it was done "with the exclusive idea of locating them in more favorable circumstances for defense."[12]

Such success as O'Conor had was made possible by the great interest and support generated by the new line of presidios and the regulations governing them. It meant that there was sufficient funding for modification of the frontier, and of importance was the regular support of Viceroy Bucareli. It is obvious that both Bucareli from the viceregal palace in Mexico City and O'Conor as his man in the field were determined to make the new plan, as earlier proposed by Rubí, a complete success. There is likewise no doubt about the level of reliance that the viceroy had on O'Conor, which was perhaps heightened by the fact that O'Conor had taken special effort to confer with Bucareli prior to his departure for the northern frontier at the beginning of his incumbency as commandant inspector.

> Though Hugo O'Conor, as Commandant-Inspector, had been sent to put into effect the new orders [the Regulations of 1772], and though he labored assiduously at his task, officials in Mexico and Spain still were not satisfied with the state of defense on the frontier, especially in the western areas, where the Apaches were more troublesome than ever. Accordingly, the Commandancy General of the Interior Provinces was created in 1776 as a potentially more effective organization for dealing with both Indians and foreign menaces to Spain's northernmost colonial provinces.[13]

O'Conor's report involves laying the foundation for eventual creation of the new administrative jurisdiction of the Interior Provinces. Though

21

11. Alfred Barnaby Thomas, *Teodoro de Croix and the Northern Frontier of New Spain* (Norman, 1941), p. 17.

12. Navarro García, *Don José de Gálvez*, p. 264.

13. Janet R. Fireman, *The Spanish Royal Corps of Engineers in the Western Borderlands: Instrument of Bourbon Reform, 1764-1815* (Glendale, 1977), p. 141.

it is in the form of a letter with the normal salutation and the equally customary closing formalities, it has elsewhere gained the title of "Papel Instructivo" or instructive report, which it certainly was meant to be. This is evident in the format, which consists of 245 separate paragraphs of greatly varying length. The Southern Methodist University manuscript does not have a paragraph 26, but a previously published Spanish version does not add such a paragraph, merely altering the enumeration. The Spanish version published in Mexico with the title *Informe de Hugo O'Conor sobre el estado de las Provincias Internas del Norte, 1771–76*[14] concludes with paragraph 243 and no closing formalities, whereas that paragraph appears as number 244 in the present manuscript, which contains two additional paragraphs plus the closing portion. There is frequent minor variation in the published *Informe*, but at no place is there any indication of the repository from which the Mexican scholars obtained their copy.

The version of the O'Conor document that we are working with is basically the same as that cited by Max Moorhead, *The Presidio*, p. 69, fn. 53 as O'Conor to Teodoro de Croix, Papel instructivo, Mexico, July 22, 1777 in the Archivo General de Indias, Guadalajara 516. Moorhead indicates that the report was enclosed with a letter from O'Conor to Minister of the Indies José de Gálvez, Mexico, July 27, 1777. Moorhead made extensive use of the document in his book, pp. 69–74.

The recipient of the O'Conor letter was a man who in large measure was innocent of any knowledge of the frontier, save by reading manuscript reports in the archives. This explains the patronizing tone of parts of O'Conor's letter, as well as the repetition of some very fundamental instructions in dealing with warfare as waged against the natives. It hardly seems necessary to have repeated some of the recommendations three times, but this might also have resulted from the fact that O'Conor did not compose his report all at once. Rather, considerable sections were made up by abstracting portions of his earlier reports. For example, paragraphs 11 through 28 and 142 through 147 of the letter to Croix are taken almost verbatim from an earlier letter by O'Conor to Viceroy Bucareli, dated 20 December 1771.[15] Paragraphs 96 through 103 are very close to what Don Hugo had reported to Bucareli on 30 January 1776.[16] Other portions of the report to Croix were adapted from a letter written to Viceroy Bucareli by O'Conor and dated 30 January 1776, at which time O'Conor was at Carrizal in Nueva Vizcaya.[17]

Teodoro de Croix at a later time indicated that O'Conor had been

14. Prologue by Lic. Enrique González Flores and notes by Francisco R. Almada (Mexico, 1952). The prologue is quite short, providing little on O'Conor as a person. The notes are almost exclusively attempts to identify place names of yesterday in terms of modern ones and are restricted almost completely to places south of the international border.

15. The letter to Bucareli is found in Rubio Mañé, "El Teniente Coronel Don Hugo O'Conor," pp. 373–90.

16. As found in Mary Lu Moore and Delmar L. Beene, "The Interior Provinces of New Spain: The Report of Hugo O'Conor, January 30, 1776," in *Arizona and the West*, vol. 13, no. 3 (Fall 1971), pp. 265–82.

17. The translated letter is available in Moore and Beene, "The Interior Provinces of New Spain," pp. 272–82. The article contains a table similar in many respects to the third table at the end of O'Conor's lengthy report to Croix, reproduced below.

unduly optimistic concerning both the status of the frontier at the time of his departure and the improvement that had been made during his time of authority. In a retrospective view of O'Conor's period seen in its best light, it would have been hard for him to instruct an uninitiated military officer, schooled in the niceties of the sophisticated warfare of European conflict, and provide him with an immediate grasp of the complexity of frontier Indian conflict against white encroachment. Once in his new post, Teodoro de Croix expected and at times received more support than O'Conor had, while at other times he felt that such support was being denied; but in either case he was not initially, if ever, as capable of getting by with limited resources.

Added to this is the change of times and of enemies. A frequent mistake by interpreters of Borderlands history is to assume "the Indian" as a more or less constant factor in the formula of frontier control. Indians, depending on the intensity and proximity of contact, viewed the intrusive Spaniards in different lights, sometimes as enemies, and at other times as friends or allies in their own struggle for control of resources. O'Conor held a rather basic, perhaps even simplistic, view. There were, as can be seen in his lengthy letter, friendly Indians. Militarily supportive ones were recruited into service in the frontier plan. Other friendly Indians served as "spies" or scouts, while still others were nonhostile, living either in missions or in Indian villages under Spanish control. Some Indians were thought to be allied with European rivals, while many others were regarded as *indios bárbaros*, literally barbarian Indians. This classification was not necessarily because they were any more barbarian than some who were friendly natives. It was because they were outside the area of Spanish control and therefore subject to persecution and chastisement. These Indians, frequently Apaches in O'Conor's writings, were the prime target of the great defense project that had been suggested by the Marqués de Rubí and instituted by Don Hugo. A less pejorative term for such Indians was *gentiles*, or non-Christians. The latter term was mostly applied to Indians who were thought to be ripe for incorporation into the mission system of native control.

The tone of O'Conor's lengthy letter was that of a person who felt that the man he was addressing was almost totally uninformed and perhaps in large measure incompetent to serve as a replacement. This might have been even more pointedly patronizing in view of the fact that Croix's appointment brought with it a great deal more power than

O'Conor had during his administration, for Croix was named as commandant general of the newly formed semi-independent unit of the Provincias Internas of New Spain. It brought Croix almost the same powers as the viceroy held in Mexico City, despite the fact that Croix had very little or no experience of Indian war. He felt no misgivings concerning his lack of preparation for his new command, rather naively exhibiting great confidence in his military skill and knowledge. A high-ranking subordinate officer, José Rubio, was given O'Conor's title of commandant inspector, serving directly under Croix. In essence the new command organization superimposed a top layer on Borderlands military structure.

If O'Conor was somewhat out of place as an Irishman on the Spanish colonial frontier and as a man whose earlier experience had included service in the European type of warfare, Frenchman Teodoro de Croix was still more out of his element. Croix was born in his ancestral castle of Prévoté near Lille at the extreme northern tip of France. Literally to the manor born, he owed his early education and preference to his noble status, and not least to the fact that his uncle was the Marqués de Croix, who was viceroy of New Spain just prior to Bucareli. Such appointments as the family enjoyed were owing to considerable French influence during the early Bourbon takeover of the crown of Spain. King Carlos III was highly impressed with French administrative skills, and the Bourbon Reforms that were initiated during the eighteenth century were in large measure concentrated in his rule.

At seventeen years of age, Teodoro entered the Spanish army and was sent to Italy, having been appointed an ensign in the Grenadiers of the Royal Guard of the army, without having gone through the normal cadetship. Three years later, in 1750, he was transferred to the Walloon Guard, with promotion to the rank of lieutenant in 1756. This unit was made up of mercenaries from southern Belgium and northern France who served the Spanish crown. In that same year in Flanders, Croix was decorated with the Cross of the Teutonic Order, from which came the title that he early used of Caballero de Croix. By 1765 he was captain of the viceregal guard and as such accompanied his uncle, the Marqués, to New Spain when that individual assumed the viceroyship in 1766. Later that same year Teodoro was appointed governor of Acapulco. According to Alfred B. Thomas, who has dealt with the younger man in his work *Teodoro de Croix and the Northern Frontier of New Spain, 1776–1783*, between December of that same year and 1770 he served as inspector of troops of New Spain and held the rank of brigadier.

Not unlike Bernardo de Gálvez, who accompanied his uncle José to Spain, Teodoro left New Spain likewise with his uncle, arriving back in Spain in 1772 after a six-month stay in Havana. Teodoro remained in Spain until 1776 when he was appointed commandant general of the new Internal Provinces. Clearly from his biographical sketch, he was ill-prepared for the type of assignment that was thrust upon him, but evidently did not lack confidence in his ability to assume the position.

Once he had arrived on the northern frontier there is reason to believe that Croix was depressed not only with his new command but also with its less than ideal state of preparedness, which he blamed on O'Conor. Moorhead indicates that "on his retirement from office, O'Conor had assured Croix that he had left the frontier companies completely equipped, mounted and provisioned," but the Irishman's successor as commandant inspector was now reporting otherwise.

Typical of the conditions in Nueva Vizcaya, according to Rubio, were those of the company at Janos. Its entire stock of firearms was either broken or rusted; its soldiers were uninstructed in the use of these weapons and, having no swords, were relying largely on lances; and its horses were undersized and undernourished. From Sonora came complaints that the company of San Bernardino was without horses, gunpowder, and musket balls, was woefully short of clothing and other necessities, and was behind in its pay; that the presidials at Tucson were without meat, butter, or candles; and that the civilian settlers at the presidio of Santa Cruz had been burned out and scattered by the Indians. The commandant inspector also reported that the paymasters were bankrupt at seven presidios and two *compañías volantes*, one having come up fifteen thousand pesos short in his accounts.[18]

18. Max L. Moorhead, *The Presidio: Bastion of the Spanish Borderlands* (Norman, 1975), p. 79.

Rather than keep the high command of the Provincias Internas in the central area that O'Conor had utilized, Croix soon transferred headquarters and therefore his capital to Arispe in northern Sonora. O'Conor had always considered Nueva Vizcaya as the nerve center of the presidial system that he had been assigned, but this was not a capricious move by Croix; rather, it was a change dictated by deterioration of the Spanish defensive position in that general area, and partially to support the recent move of the Spanish government in its quickly implemented occupation of Alta California. It is not likely that O'Conor would ever have made such a move.

In order to provide more strength to the western perimeter, Croix assigned Jacobo de Ugarte y Loyola[19] on 17 April 1780 to move the presidios of Sonora back to locations they had occupied before the Rubí recommendations and subsequent O'Conor changes. The persons responsible for the changes were Gerónimo de la Rocha y Figueroa of the Corps of Engineers and the military governor of Sonora, the aforementioned Ugarte, who was later commandant general of the Internal Provinces.

Various views of O'Conor's tenure have been presented, some contemporary and others by later interpreters of regional history. Father Juan Agustín Morfi, who served as chaplain to O'Conor's successor, Teodoro de Croix, said of the Irishman that "he did what he could, but because he lacked the necessary means, or for some other reasons beyond his power to control, he accomplished little." On other occasions Father Morfi was considerably more critical of O'Conor, as have been a number of modern historians. There have been others who have been quite laudatory of his accomplishments, resulting in a rather mixed evaluation of his activities. For example, Lawrence Kinnaird who studied the Rubí visitation said of O'Conor that after his appointment to the position of *inspector-comandante*, he undertook the duty of reorganization with great energy and courage. Kinnaird added that O'Conor's administration "was a transition period in which an attempt was made to unify the frontier provinces in a common defense."[20] Thomas, the modern historian who has been harshest in criticism of O'Conor, perhaps suffers from the weakness of many biographers by making Croix infallible and anyone who opposed him suspect of base motives or incapacity. According to Thomas, "Croix early exposed the incompetence of O'Conor, Bucareli's appointee and thereby reflected on the viceroy's judgment."[21] Croix, in turn, has had his share of detractors, such as Charles E. Chapman.[22]

Croix himself was critical of O'Conor and felt that Bucareli, as viceroy, had "an abounding confidence in the Irishman." Bucareli, in turn, was resentful of Croix's sharp criticism of O'Conor's administration. A running feud soon developed between the viceroy in his declining days and the commandant general who was hard pressed to make things work to his satisfaction. This mutual animosity did little to lighten the tremendous burdens that each had to carry.[23]

19. The story of Ugarte's participation on the northern frontier is well treated in Max L. Moorhead, *The Apache Frontier: Jacobo Ugarte and Spanish-Indian Relations in Northern New Spain, 1769–1791* (Norman, 1968). O'Conor and Ugarte did not see eye to eye concerning strategy, tactics, and policy. This was due in part to O'Conor's position of giving orders though he was junior in rank to Ugarte. Moorhead made considerable use of O'Conor's report of 1777 in his study of Ugarte.

20. Lawrence Kinnaird, *The Frontiers of New Spain: Nicolás de Lafora's Description, 1766–1768* (Berkeley, 1958), p. 41.

21. Thomas, *Teodoro de Croix* p. 29.

22. Charles E. Chapman, *A History of California: The Spanish Period* (New York, 1921), pp. 331–39.

23. Moorhead, *The Presidio*, p. 77.

After repeated requests for relief from the arduous job of defending the frontier, and on the basis of his already worsening health of which he wrote on occasions, O'Conor gave up his command in October 1776 and returned to the viceregal capital in Mexico City, rewarded by a promotion to brigadier general. He stayed there only long enough to get new orders involving his appointment to become governor and captain general of Yucatán,[24] a new position that he apparently owed to the intervention of Bucareli. His trip there took him via Jalapa to Veracruz, where after only a minimal wait he boarded a vessel for what proved to be a rough sixteen-day trip along the shores of the Bay of Campeche to the city of the same name where he arrived on 23 September. Headed along the road that followed the coast, by 10 October 1777 he was on station at Mérida. Following a pleasant changeover of command with the outgoing governor and captain general, Antonio Oliver, O'Conor settled into his new position. However, after only seventeen months of service and scarcely having become accustomed to the change from the dry and almost barren Southwest to the humid, tropical climate of Yucatán, O'Conor died there east of the city of Mérida at the Quinta de Miraflores on 8 March 1779, at age forty-four. The ascribed cause of death was overwork and fatigue, problems already apparent upon his arrival in Yucatán, and brought about by his ceaseless travels and campaigns on the northern frontier.

For a man whose public life is known in detail, we have very little by way of personal details concerning O'Conor. Apparently he never married, nor is there evidence of liaisons with women of any categories of society. When in Texas, he listed two men as resident in his household —a mule driver and a secretary. But for a person who wrote copiously, Hugo O'Conor did not permit us any easy glimpses into his private life or into his financial fortunes. That he was a brigadier by age forty-four suggests that had he lived longer, he might have achieved the highest ranks of military service. A full biography should provide us with enlightenment. It came close to realization, for the master of Borderlands research, Herbert E. Bolton, prior to his death in 1953 had as one of his future projects just such a work, for which he had already collected a substantial amount of material. Unfortunately, no later historian has taken up the challenging task of bringing O'Conor into full historical perspective.

24. Curiously, both Bobb and Thomas have O'Conor's final assignment as Guatemala.

The document translated below is from the DeGolyer Library of Southern Methodist University. It is clearly written in the hand of a scribe of the period of its origin. It offers very few paleographic problems save for some irregularities in spelling, principally of place names. To this can be added some lapses in punctuation, and at times an overabundance of commas.

29

In preparing the final translated copy, the original has been adhered to as closely as logical. O'Conor has not been given a literary capacity that was not his own, nor has great liberty been taken to change the document from its original style. Basically the *informe* appears as it would have to contemporary readers. Although O'Conor was not a native Spanish speaker, the existing document gives no evidence of lack of facility with that language.

Doubtless the writer was born O'Connor, and frequently saw his name spelled Oconor. However, I have used O'Conor except in direct quotations or where one of the other spellings seemed more appropriate. In spelling of place names, I have followed the original manuscript when such was logical, supplying present-day spelling in brackets. On a few occasions I have used the alternate spelling provided in other copies of the same or similar reports by O'Conor. There has been no attempt to identify every toponym employed in the document. Instead, some of the key places have been identified when they have had name changes in the intervening two centuries. The name El Paso has been retained from the document since it referred to the general area of the crossing of the Rio Grande, though it referred more precisely to what is today Ciudad Juárez, Chihuahua, rather than the West Texas city.

In translation of the O'Conor manuscript, I acknowledge an appreciable debt for assistance to my daughter, Andrea Cutter, a graduate of the School of Interpreters and Translators of the Universidad Autónoma de Barcelona. For any errors in the final copy, I alone am responsible. The result is a translation that conforms as closely as possible with what Hugo O'Conor said when he wrote his lengthy "instructive report" to Teodoro de Croix in 1777.

Donald C. Cutter
Albuquerque, New Mexico

Hugo O'Conor's
Report to Teodoro de Croix
July 22, 1777

My Dear Sir:

[1.] In the order that Your Lordship sent to my hands dated the 17th of last May, I find included the letter that Your Lordship seems to have sent to Chihuahua dated the 7th of the same month. In it Your Lordship says that despite the copies of my letters that His Excellency the Viceroy[1] has sent on to you, you desire that I inform you in detail of the status in which I found the frontiers of the provinces under your command; the state in which they were when I relinquished my command; and the means I think useful for successful advance of my ideas, since considering them (it is an honor that Your Lordship does me) aptly directed as a result of my knowledge and experience, Your Lordship doesn't doubt that they will serve as a guide for shaping your decisions.

[2.] I was well aware that such a report was a necessary result of the change of command, particularly for a leader such as Your Lordship who has not seen the lands of which it is comprised, even though you may possess fully as much information as given by someone with the most perfect theory, but since many of Your Lordship's measures arrived there in advance of your appointment, and even much before my departure, I reasoned on that basis that either Your Lordship did not need the information which you ask me to supply for you, or that my work would be fruitless no matter how much I might be animated by the belief of its usefulness, or by a desire to please Your Lordship and by the advantages to the service.

[3.] These thoughts, which were a partial cause of my inaction up to now, I have then added to the slights that the reports of my experiences would probably suffer in view of the orders you have already issued for the frontier, perhaps because you have preferred those reports that in Your Lordship's ideas and opinions were more solid, and in truth I do not understand how this fits in with the honor that is bestowed on me in your writing of wanting to use my rules as a guide for your measures when so many have already been issued without having heard from me.

1. The Bailio Frey Don Antonio María Bucareli y Ursúa was the viceroy and he and O'Conor had a close professional association. The viceroy had been born in Sevilla on 24 January 1717 and died in office in Mexico City on 9 April 1779, just one month after O'Conor's death. He is considered to have been one of the best to hold that office. On his important role as viceroy see Bernard E. Bobb, *The Viceregency of Antonio María Bucareli in New Spain, 1771-1779* (Austin, 1962).

[4.] Thus confirmed, from what I can expect of Your Lordship's acceptance, I should refrain from giving my judgment on a matter concerning which my opinion is so little esteemed and even more so from reporting what I think practicable for the gradual continuation of my successful ideas, as I am certain those of Your Lordship are contrary and different in everything, perhaps because in carrying them out you expect better results, and I will certainly rejoice in them because I desire the advancement of the service and Your Lordship's gratification.

[5.] Nevertheless, motivated by my own good inclination to cooperate in these because of my esteem for Your Lordship and because, in addition to the service of the King, some provinces, the lands of which I have trod, forsaking fatigue, and the security of which I have sought at the cost of many risks and hardships by whatever my zeal for the service animated me to and the love which I profess for them inspired me to, deserve all of mine, I will make for Your Lordship a detailed report of what occurred during the period of my command in case the events, measures, and other things I will mention might serve Your Lordship for knowledge even if not for their wisdom.

[6.] At the end of the year 1771 Captain Don Bernardo de Gálvez[2] was in command of the troops of Nueva Vizcaya. When the government decided to relieve him so that he could return to Spain with his uncle, the Illustrious Señor José de Gálvez,[3] this position with 2,000 pesos in additional pay or expense allowance was entrusted to me by decree of 10 September.

[7.] When I received said order, I already knew that the present Lord Viceroy Frey Don Antonio Bucareli y Ursúa was on his way to this capital, sent to succeed His Excellency Señor Marqués de Croix,[4] and as it seemed to me proper to await his arrival in case besides those already given, he had any other bits of advice to give me, I proceeded in that way, convinced that everything worked together to guarantee the success of such an important commission.

[8.] With this desire, I reported to the new viceroy three days after his arrival. I delivered to him the said order and on his being informed of its contents, he not only approved the measures of his predecessor, but also, dated 4 October of that same year, he notified me in an order of

2. Bernardo de Gálvez was the nephew of Visitor General José de Gálvez. He served as commander of the military forces of Nueva Vizcaya, subsequently as Governor of Louisiana, and later as Viceroy of New Spain. O'Conor spoke highly of him in this report, but in letters that would not reach the highest circles he was critical of Don Bernardo. Details of his life can be found in John W. Caughey, *Bernardo de Gálvez in Louisiana, 1776–1783* (Berkeley, 1934).

3. In 1765 José de Gálvez was sent to New Spain by the crown as visitor general with powers superior to those of the viceroy, the Marqués de Cruillas. Part of Gálvez's six-year stay was spent in military campaigns in Sonora. He returned to Spain and became Minister of the Indies with the title Marqués de Sonora. The best-documented treatment of his role is Luis Navarro García, *Don José de Gálvez y la Comandancia General de las Provincias Internas del Norte de Nueva España* (Sevilla, 1964).

4. The Marqués de Croix succeeded Cruillas as Viceroy and has been categorized as "a complaisant friend of the visitor" general, José de Gálvez. Appointed in 1766, he served until 1771 and during this time he issued the instructions for formation of the line of presidios.

his own of the importance of my transfer to Chihuahua, strictly charging me with the fulfillment of that command on the condition of giving reports by mail of everything that might happen.

9. Having prepared my journey, I moved to the city of Chihuahua where I was to take command of the frontier, and although I arrived there on 17 December of that year, I could not do so until the 19th because of Captain Don Bernardo Gálvez being on campaign.

10. I devoted myself immediately to getting acquainted with the status of the provinces under my command and particularly that of Nueva Vizcaya, and I learned that it more than all the others was greatly disturbed by the continual incursions of the Apaches, which terror reached the utmost. When I felt that I had full information, I informed the government of the nature of the evils suffered by that province and of the deplorable, fatal state to which I found it reduced since the year 1748, during which time persistent war continued, with the Apaches almost always gaining complete victory in what they attempted; and with the King losing an abundance of property, leaving ineffectual the measures and efforts of the government and with scant honor to His Majesty's troops.

11.[5] The narrative of the destruction, robberies, deaths, and other types of damage that I then reported would seem at first glance too exaggerated either as the result of fear or of special purposes of the informants, but besides being based on their reality, they are all evident in very trustworthy documents that I have left in the Archive of Chihuahua.

12. Irrefutable and visible proofs of this truth are the Indian and Spanish towns: Guarachi, San Juan, San Antonio, Santa Rita, Santa Rosa, Namiquipa, Las Cruces, and San Luis located to the north and west of the city of Chihuahua; the valley of Santa Clara, the rich haciendas of Casas Grandes, Torreón de Amoloya [Almoloya], Las Cruces, San Miguel Namiquipa, Babicora, El Picacho, El Rincón de Zerna, San Luis, Malanoche, La Laguna de Pacheco, Agua Nueva, Hormigas, El Torreón de Guemes, El Sacramento, Las Chorreras, and many ranchos that there were nearby, all of which were found totally depopulated because their inhabitants had not been able to resist the continual invasions of the barbarians.[6]

5. This paragraph and those following through paragraph 28 were taken by O'Conor from a letter that he had much earlier written to Viceroy Bucareli from Chihuahua on 20 December 1771. The letter in its entirety appears in the *Boletín del Archivo General de la Nación* 30, pp. 371–91.

6. The Spanish word used in this and other documents is *bárbaros* or *indios bárbaros*, which I have translated as barbarians. It had a political rather than strictly cultural meaning. Most historians have used it as a synonym for enemy.

13. The valley of San Buenaventura, garrisoned formerly by detachments of presidial soldiers and later by the presidio of the same name, had its agricultural assets totally destroyed and was abandoned by the inhabitants that populated it because of their having sought safety in flight. The Hacienda de Carmen, whose crops and horse herds could not escape the hands of the Indians, I found reduced to a very poor small field, since it did not have enough mules for transporting and selling its crops. That of Carrizal, which was always supported by government order with a detachment for its defense, nevertheless suffered almost the same fate. And the Haciendas de Encinillas, at which previously there had been more than 46,000 cattle, only had about 8,000 due to repeated robbery and destruction by the barbarians.

14. With good cause, the inhabitants of those towns and valleys bemoaned this, with the main role taken by the big hacenderos and ranch owners since the number of their cattle reached over 300,000 head, that of their minor livestock 200,000 head, and that of the horse and mule herds about 400,000, because most of the haciendas were for breeding and had high sales and consumption in the areas of silver exploitation. They then had scarcely a third.

15. To the east and south of Chihuahua [city] various haciendas and settlements were also found abandoned. Those of El Sauz, 16 leagues from that city, where I was lodged the day before arriving there, had just suffered one of the many attacks that the Indians were in the habit of committing. When they did not find any people there, as evidence of their ferocity and as a release of their vengeance they broke down the doors, entered it at will, and destroyed desks, tables, chairs, a box of vestments, the chapel and all the furniture that they found in it. That of San Antonio de la Javonera, that of Ozes [Hoces], that of Sapiain, that of El Belduque, La Boca del Potrero de Domínguez, the town of San Pedro de Julimes, and the valley of Basuchil suffered likewise, and in the latter were found abandoned the haciendas of San Ignacio, of San Antonio de Padua, San Juan, and various ranchos of numerous inhabitants along the banks of the Conchos, Florido, and San Pedro rivers who lost all of their assets and, for many, also their lives. The valley of San Nicolás had likewise been depopulated of two-thirds of its inhabitants, and the remaining third was making ready to do the same out of justifiable fear of losing everything.

16. Those evils extended as far as the valley of San Bartolomé that is 60 leagues from the city of Chihuahua. I was there when I made my entrance into the Provincias Internas, and at the Hacienda de Santa Cruz de los Neyras I was assured by its owner that the enemies had already made an end to all his agricultural property, reducing the very little he had left to the enclosure of his house, since it was safe. These [evils] also extended to the Real del Parral[7] that is 70 leagues from the city and to the Hacienda Apantita and the town of Mapimí, the former close to the relocated Presidio de El Gallo, where on 30 August in the stated year of [17]71, five people were killed; and even as far as the Río Nazas, taking from the Hacienda de San Salvador de Orta all the mules and over 300 horses and with the death of five servants. But the many people, regardless of sex or age, who have suddenly lost their lives to the cruelty of the barbarians, were the object of greater compassion. Young babies were torn to bits at the breasts of their mothers and even in their wombs, carrying out on the dead bodies the most detestable excesses of ferocity and cruelty. This was sufficient motive that it stimulated the Christian zeal of His Excellency to assert his justice with due punishment for such serious crimes.

7. Today, Hidalgo del Parral, Chihuahua.

17. In the years [17]71 and [17]72 at the Hacienda del Mayorazgo more than 30 people were killed; the minor livestock was greatly destroyed, taking with them all the horse and mule herd that they found; and since the hacienda was already abandoned the Mayorazgo retired to Parral, leaving this family greatly in debt. The same number of deaths was caused in the place called El Durazno, close to the Río de Conchos. In the canyon of Cusiguriachi [Cosiguiriachi] five drivers were killed of a mule train that was going there from this city loaded with merchandise, a large portion of which was taken and also the pack mules. At the Presidio de Janos a goodly number of barbarians killed 11 soldiers and five friendly Indians, seizing from them over 500 horses of the garrison. From the Hacienda de Dolores belonging to the church assets, and from some neighbors, over 1,000 head of horses and mules were taken. One league from the city of Chihuahua at the Hacienda de Tabalaopa, also belonging to the church assets, six people and some 200 head of minor livestock were killed just to do damage to anything of any use. At the Cañada de Jugo two leagues from the city, they took the lives of five people. They immediately went on to the Hacienda de Bachimba and did the same with another seven, finding no opposition from its forces.

They later struck the Hacienda de San Antonio de la Javonera where they cruelly killed 16 people between men, women, and children, leaving it completely depopulated. From there they went to the Camino Real de Mexico and hit a string of 21 groups of mules loaded with merchandise belonging to various interested parties and along with it the tobacco for the royal tobacco monopoly. Of the 90 men between owners, escorts, and mule drivers that were carrying this load, seven were killed and the rest were forced to retreat, frightened by the superior multitude of their enemies. Once in possession of everything, the Indians opened over 170 bundles of clothing, tobacco, and other merchandise. The result of such destruction was considerable havoc, since having loaded up what they liked, they scattered the remainder over a distance of seven leagues: as a result, when later assessing the damage, including the complete loss of mules, saddles and equipment, the loss exceeded 30,000 pesos.

18. On another occasion they attacked the New Mexico pack train some two leagues from the city, taking at that time some 1,000 horses and mules, after having left seven lifeless people. On its return such a large number of Indians attacked it that our men numbering some 320, after six hours of spirited resistance, only managed to kill three Indians, wound two, and take from them the groups of horses and mules that they were taking off to their lands. An equal multitude of barbarians appeared at the Rancho del Potrero, where they did not leave anyone alive, with three boys and six girls, of which children the eldest was seven years old and the youngest four months, losing their lives in this general surprise attack, a circumstance that sufficiently demonstrates the ferocity of the Indians, as they do not even spare the most defenseless innocents. Their tyranny does not cease here, but goes on to include pregnant women, opening their wombs with the greatest cruelty. Their inhumanities certainly cannot be referred to without offending modesty and decency.

19. En route I learned that on 11 October of that same year they had carried off from the vicinity of the city of Chihuahua and the Real de Santa Eulalia about 600 horses and mules, and killed 10 men of the 14 who went out in pursuit of them. Don Bernardo de Gálvez was wounded, though slightly, by five enemy Indians whom he met when he had gone out to catch up with the squad.

20. A few days before my arrival they struck a second blow, carrying off the horses and mules that the miners still had. Bernardo de Gálvez set out in pursuit with 125 buckskin-clad soldiers,[8] 150 Indians of the Opata nation and other friends, the captain of Julimes Don Manuel Muñoz,[9] and that of San Buenaventura Don Nicolás Gil. The commander returned with 45 men, and the others continued on the trail of those enemies, but without achieving the purpose of their efforts.

21. After my arrival in the city of Chihuahua and before taking command of its frontiers for the reasons that I explained to the Most Excellent Lord Viceroy in letters of 22 November and 13 December of the year [17]71, they killed on the Janos road a nephew of the captain of that very presidio and two soldiers who were coming for medicine for the sick captain, who died, as I reported to His Excellency. From the Hacienda de la Natividad of Don Luis de Ulibarri, they carried off all the horses and mules, doing the same thing at that time in the valley of San Bartolomé where they killed a muleteer and carried off a young man, who with three others that they also wounded was carrying some loads of wheat to the city. On the banks of the Río San Pedro, they killed seven Indian fishermen. On the Río Conchos, I was told that an enemy Indian scout had inflicted five lance wounds on another Indian from the town who died within three hours of receiving the Holy Sacraments. There was news of another three persons who had died at the hands of those barbarians near the Real de Cusiguriachi, so that within the first 15 days of my stay in the city, besides the robberies, there were already not a few deaths.

22. It would extend this report too much to repeat the innumerable public and notorious deeds of this nature in all the settlements, haciendas, ranchos, and roads of the province of Nueva Vizcaya. I have only detailed some as examples of what was happening so you can form a positive idea of the many fatalities suffered by the inhabitants of these lands due to the almost daily cruelty, deaths, and robberies that were perpetrated by the barbarians, sometimes in one place, sometimes in another, with very little loss to their squads.

23. By understanding the desertion of entire settlements; the depopulation of haciendas and ranchos; the destruction of the herds of horses, mules, cattle, and minor livestock; the repeated killing of soldiers, cit-

39

8. The ubiquitous leather-jacketed soldier is treated by Max Moorhead in "The Soldado de Cuera: Stalwart of the Spanish Borderlands," in Oakah L. Jones, Jr. (ed.), *The Spanish Borderlands: A First Reader* (Los Angeles, 1974), pp. 87–105.

9. From 1776 to 1783 Manuel Muñoz was commander of presidios of the Rio Grande. In 1777 he was made lieutenant colonel of cavalry of Nueva Vizcaya. In 1780 he was colonel and interim governor of that same province, and in 1785 he was again interim governor of Nueva Vizcaya.

izens, travelers, and servants; the loss of everyone's assets; and the total loss of the fortunes of many, since from the month of January of the said year of [17]71 until 20 December of the same year alone, there were 150 deaths, 16 who escaped wounded, an equal number captured, and 7,000 horses and mules stolen, not counting the cattle destroyed; and calculating at the time of war according to prudent opinions of the most thoughtful people, the number of dead of one sex or the other exceeded 4,000 at the hands of the barbarians and the loss of all the merchandise totaled over 12,000,000 [pesos], the state of the province of [Nueva] Vizcaya can clearly be deduced. [There has been a] decline of its commerce since interested parties did not dare to send their goods, prudently fearing their loss, nor do the owners of the mule trains dare to bring them in, with similar misgivings concerning their lives and mules; the scarcity of supplies for the same reason and even of coal and firewood, as the people who carried it, being more defenseless, were more exposed to losing their lives, as is shown by the repeated examples.

24. The decline of the mines has been obvious and of considerable importance since the use of mules is indispensable for the exploitation of their metals, as they cannot be transported in any other way to the haciendas, nor broken up nor ground, and due to the lack of mules there has been a big delay both in the transporting of those metals and of the fluxing ingredients, as well as in that of coal for the foundries and of necessary supplies for the operators. As a result, with the exception of one or another hacienda that had facilities for taking water, the rest have stopped because of the continual theft of animals. All of which are reasons that inspired the memorials made to the Government by the delegates of that body of miners and of commerce.

25. I cannot omit the important thought that since this province had its beginnings in the year [170]7 of this century, until that of [17]48 only 41 years have passed; and in that short time it achieved such well-known growth in cities, mining camps, towns, valleys, haciendas, and other smaller settlements, which made it most profitable in comparison to all of the internal [provinces] of this kingdom, contributing to the greater increase of the Royal Treasury, enriching many individuals, providing comforts and the hope of greater gain to its inhabitants and extending its commerce as far as this city and to the most important ones of the kingdom and giving rise to many riches in the Provincias Internas. All

of these are reasons why its population was the greatest, gathered together there because of its wealth and without expense to the King our Lord. Although the war began in the year [17]48 lasting until 20 December [17]71, waged with continued tenacity for 23 years since the time of the aforementioned prosperity, it gave rise to the well-known backwardness. The same mines exist as in the beginning because this land has enjoyed the advantageous circumstance of never flooding. Among them are many of gold and silver that offer great riches and they could be enjoyed fully if the people there, and those who could be congregated, managed to live at ease and work without the imminent risk of losing their assets and lives in the continual invasions of the barbarians.

[There is no paragraph 26.]

27. Proof of this truth is the presence in the city of Chihuahua of miners who reached the point of sending shipments of up to 100 silver bars, but in the year [17]71 the shipment that went out from there was so small that there were among them some who could not send even one. Despite this notable difference there arrived in this capital 608 bars, from which it can be inferred that the province of [Nueva] Vizcaya, free of the hostilities of such continuous and cruel warfare, such as it has suffered and that no other would have suffered for such a long time without ending in total destruction, is not only sufficient to enrich itself, and make its residents happy with what it can produce, but also to increase the commerce of all the kingdom with evident benefits to the Royal Treasury in alcabalas, quintos, assays, and other lawful contributions.

28. Nor can I help but note that this province is a conduit for commerce and communication with New Mexico and Sonora, Tarahumara, Sinaloa, Nayarit, Pimería Alta and Baja, with many settlements, presidios, and missions at which they deal with the conversion of many nations. With the passage of time and with the intrusion of the barbarians and its depopulation making roads impassible, it would be necessary that either there be indispensably increased expenses for its correction or that all be lost or abandoned.

29. In the city of Chihuahua a company of 60 buckskin-clad soldiers, 25 Norteño Indians, and 21 Janchez was maintained. The former each

get 20 pesos monthly pay and the others get 10. There are 41 men including the captain, lieutenant, ensign, sergeant, and four squadron corporals in a detachment at the Presidio de Cerro Gordo, distant about 100 leagues south of the city of Chihuahua; 40 men including the officers at the Presidio de Guaxuquilla,[10] 70 leagues distant from the city in the same direction as the preceding one; 50 men, counting the officers, at the Presidio de Julimes, 22 leagues from the city; 50 men at the Presidio de San Buenaventura, 70 leagues distant to the north; and 50 at that of Janos, 95 leagues distant in the same direction. Thus in this vast province there are 336 soldiers including the presidial detachments, the buckskin-clad ones, and the Indians of the Norteño and Janche nations.

30. To form a body of troops for the campaigns that were carried out, it was necessary to break up those presidios, taking squads away from all. To these were added Indians of the Opata nation and other friends, with which the number rose to over 300 men with the exception of the first campaign carried out by Don Lope de Cuellar,[11] which reached 700 because of having had an order to raise a body of recruits that was soon reconstituted and, as I understand, without either an order or a decree of this superior government, nor even with consent of the Illustrious Señor Don José de Gálvez, under whose superior orders the aforementioned Cuellar was.

31. While the first campaign of Don Lope de Cuellar was going on, the Indians struck the Pueblo de San Gerónimo, 5 leagues distant from the city of Chihuahua, killing 49 persons including men, women, and children, and capturing 11. Three days later they struck at the mission of Nombre de Dios, one league distant from that city, with eight individuals dying at their evil hands.

32. During the second [campaign] they attacked the Hacienda de la Javonera, at which hardly anyone was left alive. Immediately thereafter on the Camino Real they destroyed 21 bundles of a commercial shipment, with the death of seven drovers and loss of the mules.

33. During the third [campaign] they struck in the valley of San Bartolomé and Hacienda de Bachimba, resulting in 11 persons dead and 10 captives, in addition to more than 3,000 and some odd horses and mules that they carried off.

10. Variously spelled Guajoquilla and Huajuquilla, it is today Ciudad Jiménez, Chihuahua.

11. Lope de Cuellar, following the expulsion of the Jesuit order from New Spain, was appointed civil governor of Tarahumara Alta, Tarahumara Baja, and Tepehuanes. He served as governor of Nueva Vizcaya from 1768 to 1773. See Oakah L. Jones, Jr., *Nueva Vizcaya: Heartland of the Spanish Frontier* (Albuquerque, 1988), p. 177.

34. During the fourth campaign that went out on 6 September [17]71 and returned on 28 October of the same year, they caused 28 deaths, wounded several, and carried off more than 1,700 animals; and repeating with a second sortie they carried off the mules that the miners still had left, being the reason why work ceased at most of the silver workings, with notable disadvantages to their owners and to the community.

35. Concerning everything expressed up to this point, it is every way evident that with the 291 armed men there were in the province they could not prevent the robberies, deaths, and destruction by the enemies; nor contain them in their continual attacks; nor teach them a lesson with the proper punishment that their haughtiness, daring, and cruelty deserved.

36. During the brief time that he was commander of the frontier, Don Bernardo de Gálvez dedicated himself to the achievement of such an important objective, with that valiant officer not sparing hardships, lack of sleep, nor risks that might lead to the achievement of his laudable designs, giving an example to his troop of the valor and constancy that such a strange war requires, as is evident by the fact of that officer having received various wounds in the different engagements that he had with the enemies.

37. According to the reports of its governor, the province of Coahuila was under attack by the Mescalero Apaches, and on its frontier the Presidio de San Juan Bautista del Río Grande del Norte, Monclova, Santa Rosa del Sacramento, as well as that of San Sabá, which by government order was assigned to the Villa de San Fernando de Austria, in the status of "until further orders"; and although with this force the haughtiness of the Mescaleros could have been curbed, it has not been accomplished as a result of the shameful inaction of this troop which the Most Excellent Marqués Señor de Rubí knew well, and so stated in the note that is found in his "general opinion," giving the term "rusty" to the arms of this province, in order to point out the little use that was made of them.

38. From Sonora there was frequent news of the hostilities committed on its frontier by the Apaches living in the intricate and extended Sierra de Chiricagui.[12] To rid it of those dangers there are the following pre-

12. Today it is spelled Chiricahua and the southwestern Apaches resident in that area of southeastern Arizona are likewise so called.

sidios: Fronteras, Terrenate, Tubac, Santa Gertrudis del Altar, San Miguel de Horcasitas, Buenavista, and a mobile company. The garrison of each of its presidios consists of a captain, lieutenant, ensign, sergeant, four corporals, and 42 buckskin-clad privates. But the latter unit has no officers because of being attached to the Presidio de Terrenate and under the orders of its captain, Joseph Antonio de Vildósola.[13]

13. Characterized by John L. Kessell, *Friars, Soldiers, and Reformers: Hispanic Arizona and the Sonora Mission Frontier, 1767–1856* (Tucson, 1976), pp. 73–74, as imperious and hot-headed, José Antonio de Vildósola later was rapidly promoted to colonel through the intervention of Teodoro de Croix. He became military commandant of Sonora in 1782, succeeding Jacobo de Ugarte.

39. In New Mexico the Comanches make their attacks from the north and the Gileño Apaches from the west. In that province there is a presidio of 80 men, including the captain, who is also its governor, two lieutenants, an ensign, and two sergeants, and a numerous citizenry capable of its own defense, both because of its great number as well as the proven military spirit and valor that its individuals possess.

40. The province of Texas has the presidios named Nuestra Señora del Pilar de los Adaes, with 60 men including officers; San Agustín de Ahumada with 31 men, including the captain, a lieutenant, and a sergeant; La Bahía del Espíritu Santo with 50 men including the captain, lieutenant, ensign, and a sergeant; and that of San Antonio de Béxar, whose complement is composed of a captain, sergeant, two corporals, and 19 buckskin-clad privates. Notwithstanding, its lands were continually attacked by the warlike and numerous nations of the north, concerning whose numbers and circumstances I will speak in the proper place, as well as of the vast lands that comprise this beautiful jewel.

41. When the government heeded the trustworthy and repeated reports about the hostilities that the indicated northern nations committed in the vicinity of the Presidio de San Antonio de Béxar, Villa de San Fernando, and the five opulent missions that in the short distance of three leagues are located on the Río San Antonio, by a decree issued in the month of February or March of the past year of [17]70 it decided upon the transfer of the Presidio de San Agustín de Ahumada to that of San Antonio de Béxar, reinforcing that garrison with a lieutenant and 20 privates from that of San Sabá, so that with these forces and with the aid of the mission Indians, the governor would not only have enough to prevent the hostilities that the enemies commit in the nearby lands, but also have a fully sufficient force to pursue them and punish them in their own rancherias. To carry it out some rifles and munitions of war

were sent, although as I understand it they profited little from these measures because of the lack of use that was made of them.

42. The Most Excellent Marqués de Rubí[14] in his prudent report, which Your Lordship will find in the Archive of Chihuahua, describes with considerable propriety and aptness the little or no utility that the service experienced from the old presidial locations, their internal management, and the perverse fraud with which the paltry salary of the soldiers was handled. He points out the latitude in which the presidios were located, and everything else that he indicates in his reviews makes clear the change that was needed. Therefore I consider it fruitless to go on when through his experiences rather than mine you can deduce the aptness with which the new Royal Instruction was formed for governing the troops and presidios under Your Lordship's command.

43. This was the state in which I found the Provincias Internas when I took command of them, and believing that I have fully satisfied the first point of Your Lordship's letter of 17 May, I will now treat the measures that were subsequently taken in view of my reports, although with the misgiving of forgetting some essentials because all the documents that contain them are in Chihuahua and it is necessary to depend on memory.

14. Cayetano María Pignatelli Rubí Corbera y San Climent, the Marqués de Rubí, came to New Spain in November 1764 with the Villalba expedition for the reorganization of the military forces of New Spain. To that end, Rubí was assigned to carry out a military inspection of the frontier, one in which O'Conor was a participant in the Texas phase. From this inspection, the oft-cited *dictamen*, or opinion, of the Marqués resulted. Rubí forwarded his *dictamen* to Minister of the Indies Julián de Arriaga from Veracruz on 4 May 1768. Apparently there were several copies, one of which was in the archives in Chihuahua. See Lawrence Kinnaird, *The Frontiers of New Spain: Nicolás de Lafora's Description, 1766–1768* (Berkeley, 1958).

Measures of the Council of War and Royal Treasury of 2 April 1772

44. I always felt that the sad news of so many evils would take by surprise the attention of the Lord Viceroy who is dedicated to making those provinces happy, and that if very firm and quick measures were not taken this end could not be achieved, with the King risking what was left in them. Actually, by common accord in the said meeting, the removal of the presidios of Julimes, Cerro Gordo, San Sabá, Santa Rosa, and Monclova was resolved—the first to the junction of the Río del Norte

and the Conchos, which name [la Junta] it now bears and where it was formerly located; and the other four along the banks of the Río Grande del Norte in all of the land that there is of some 150 leagues from the former [presidio] to San Juan Bautista, so as to cover the frontiers of the provinces of [Nueva] Vizcaya and Coahuila, and according to what was also decided in the new project and regulation for location of presidios along the line [of presidios]. The corresponding orders were given to me so that once the governors of those provinces had carefully inspected the broad, fertile, and most appropriate places, presidios would be located at equal or proportionate distances, performing the other duties and inspections that are called for in chapters 19, 20, 21, and 22 of said regulations regarding the new establishment of the four relocated presidios.

45. Copies were sent to us for our information and guidance, with a warning that if through absence or legitimate obstacle of the governors of Coahuila and Nueva Vizcaya, they could not agree on the reconnaissance of the places closest to those seats of government in which the four transferable presidios ought to be located, I would do it by myself or [have it done] by well informed persons whom I would commission for the purpose.

46. That as established in the aforementioned regulation, there be assigned and delivered to the captain of the five transferable presidios, the amount of 3,000 pesos to pay the cost of new construction of the enclosure that each one should occupy in the place to be indicated to them, where in order that construction be according to the new plan, the square of common adobe walls should be built first with the two small bastions at its corners, later erecting in the interior the chapel, guardhouse, captain's house, and rooms for the soldiers and friendly Indians and scouts, all taking shelter in the meanwhile in tents and provisional barracks. The delivery of those 3,000 pesos was ordered by royal officials of this capital to be disbursed to the agents and suppliers that the captains of those presidios had there, under the customary guarantee of presenting the corresponding account of its distribution.

47. That in case in the places where the presidios that were to be moved were formerly located, the families and inhabitants that had been there should remain, for their protection and defense the existing physical

fortifications would remain, but in case they should also move along with the troop of those presidios to their new locations, they were to be demolished, tearing them down completely to avoid the enemy making use of them in any encounter or pursuit our troops may make of them.

48. That the Presidio de San Antonio de Béxar have its garrison increased as was proposed in the new regulation, up to the number of 80 billets, composed of a captain, two lieutenants, an ensign, a chaplain, two sergeants, and 73 corporals and privates, but with the enjoyment of the current salaries those officers and other individuals of that presidio then had.

49. That not only the 60 men of the Chihuahua company be increased to 100, but also another three of equal number be raised from the people of the area, as was proposed, in order that the first with 45 friendly Indian scouts that it currently has might be used in containing the attacks of the enemy on the roads and at agricultural haciendas, so that with this help the mines of the Real de Santa Eulalia might be worked and so the haciendas near this city might exploit its silver with some ease. The other three [companies] could be used for the same purpose when necessity might require, and more especially to expel the enemy from the location of Agua Nueva and other [locations] where at greater distances it might be necessary to station them. And also so that while moving the above-mentioned presidios to their new locations, they might reconnoiter and protect the broad land that there was in between, from the location where they were to those that were to be occupied, so the enemy will not remain behind their backs, and they might hurl them to the other side of the Río Grande del Norte, without for any reason allowing the Lipan Apaches to remain in the district of Coahuila.

50. That the four mobile companies of 100 men be composed of a captain, with the salary of 100 pesos a month; of two lieutenants with that of 50; two ensigns with 40; two sergeants with 24; four corporals with 22; and 89 privates with 20 pesos each.

51. That to each of the three that should be newly formed, there be added 25 friendly Indian scouts with a salary of 3 reales daily, with the 45 that already existed remaining in that of Chihuahua with the salary which up to then they enjoyed.

52. That there be named two principal adjutants for the functions of that office in the districts into which they were divided and they be assigned to those companies with the salary of 55 pesos a month each, from which they should pay for the armament of shotguns, lances, shields, and leather jackets, and giving to them on the King's account the six horses and a mule which were furnished for each one under the old presidio ordinances, since with their salaries they could not bear the cost because of the high price of arms and clothing materials in those lands.

53. That since the officers and principal adjutants of those four mobile companies must be subjects of valor, aptitude, and experience in the enemy Indian way of waging war, and knowledgeable of their ideas and cunning, and of the places in which they usually lie in ambush and take refuge, they should propose through me to this captaincy generalship the people they consider most fitting, while at the same time taking care that the recruits enlisted for the formation of the mobile companies be useful and valiant people, and that they should have knowledge of the lands and of the enemy Indians so that their service be of honor to the nation and utility to the state.

54. That in the interim while His Majesty was deciding about creation of the line of presidios proposed by the Excellent Lord Marqués de Rubí and the naming of general officers and an inspector that are called for in the regulation written during the time of the Lord Marqués de Croix for the government of the presidios located on the line, I was named as Comandante General of the troops of Chihuahua and the rest of the frontier, and in consideration of the work and of travel and campaign expenses, there was assigned to me the annual allowance of 2,000 pesos in addition to the salary of 600 that I enjoyed as captain of the Presidio de San Sabá.

55. In view of the fact that in the status report I sent in with my letter of 18 February about the number of people that comprise the Chihuahua company, I stated that the troop currently there was without armament, which indicated the poverty of their arms, they promptly sent 550 carbines or shotguns appropriate for cavalry, an equal number of swords with their scabbards, and the number of flints and balls that were considered enough to serve for the period of a year, not only for this com-

pany, but also for the three [companies] of 100 men that were to be formed. From the office of royal accounts there has been sent to me a memorandum concerning the value of those arms, flints, and balls, with notice of the freightage, so that by dividing it among the individuals of the four companies, the amount be discounted from their respective salaries because they have to defray it, and also indicating to me that in case the friendly Indians and scouts do not use shotguns and swords, but do use lances and pikes, the remainder may be sold on behalf of the Royal Treasury to the citizens of Chihuahua who may want to buy them for their use and for the defense of their homes and property.

56. Mindful that at His Majesty's expense each of the soldiers of the interior presidios was given yearly six pounds of powder for training and for military operations against the barbarians, it was ordered to provide each individual of the four mobile companies with an equal number of pounds and that the cost to the supply officers be sent promptly at His Majesty's expense and that in the interim until it arrives at said city, they will supply from the office of royal accounts what was needed for those troops on the condition of repayment of the principal cost, as well as the freight to Chihuahua, to the administration of this [military] department.

57. That for the payments to those four companies and the friendly Indians attached to them, and for the salary of the commandant general, adequate funds be sent at the beginning of each year. That they apply the 5,000 pesos left over because of paying in four years the 25,000 of redemption of the Presidio del Pasage, and the surplus each year from the presidios and sales tax from the city of Chihuahua, as well as the total of the grains of silver with which those miners contribute, all of which amounted to 12,000 pesos annually.

58. That in order to defray promptly the payments to the troops during the aforementioned first year of [17]72 and the purchase of horses and mules with which they should be provided, there be issued by the Most Excellent Lord Viceroy the corresponding order to the intendant of Sonora, Don Pedro Corbalán,[15] to send without losing a moment and with a suitable escort for its safe transport, the 100,000 pesos in cash that was sent from the treasury of that capital [Mexico City] to that province [of Sonora] and which it was reported was held up in the Real

15. As intendant of Sonora for many years, Pedro de Corbalán's name appears frequently in the regional records. The 100,000 pesos had been sent to Sonora to purchase unminted gold that was thought to have been in great abundance in the gold mining boom at Cieneguilla. Much material on Corbalán is found in Navarro García, *Don José de Gálvez*.

del Pitic because of not having been able to use them in exchange for the silver and gold bullion for which they had been sent.

59. Since it was necessary that in the city of Chihuahua there be a person to perform the functions of war commissary and treasurer and to carry out the monthly review of the four companies of 100 men and of the Indians attached to them and that in conformity with the extract of the reviews, he formalize the payment of their salaries, paying monthly or every third of a year the sum of them, there was appointed by me a proper person for everything, who was to keep formal accounts with the requirement of presenting them to the Royal Tribunal [of Accounts] at the proper times. As a result he was assigned 2,000 pesos salary for himself, and 400 for the scribe who would aid him, bonded in advance up to the sum of 10,000 pesos.

60. That in the interim until a person be named who would serve in this position, the corregidor of that city should hold the monthly reviews of the troops in which its commander would participate, and in case of his illness or absence, the captain or highest ranking officer of that troop, and in conformity with those inspections payments would be made in cash in accordance with the assigned salaries, so that in this way the troop may enjoy them, buying with it what was needed and also so there could be made from it the respective deductions for the value of the arms that should be received on His Majesty's account.

61. That taking into account the savings to the Royal Treasury, if be made available the amount of the annual allowance of the four mentioned presidios of Los Adaes, San Agustín de Ahumada, Monterrey, and Mesa del Tonatí in Nayarit that by the new regulations were ordered suppressed, and taking into account that it all adds up to 64,208 pesos and a few *tomines*,[16] it could help cover a large part of the growing costs that the said measures would entail. But also taking into account the frequent reports of havoc, deaths, and robberies that the Apaches continued to commit everywhere, and that suppression of those four presidios could give them more room and freedom for their attacks, while at the same time it was possible to prevent it from happening, I was ordered that once well informed of the status of said presidios in their present locations, and that of the lands attacked by the Indians, I report whether it would be worthwhile that they be maintained in the places

16. A *tomín* was approximately the eighth part of a peso or 12-1/2 cents.

where they are located or that they all or some of them be suppressed. Moreover, if I considered their permanence necessary for waging better warfare everywhere on the barbarian, I was not to make any changes in them.

62. That in case I considered suppression of the presidios of Los Adaes, San Agustín de Ahumada, and Monterrey necessary, it should be done promptly, keeping at the first its governor with the salary that he was assigned so he might administer justice in the province. And if the second [San Agustín] be carried out, an equal amount; but if there is also the suppression of Monterrey, that there remain in it, notwithstanding, the governor and the chaplain with the garrison of soldiers in addition to a squad of eight men, each with an annual salary of 200 pesos that the regulation also provides for.

63. It was also decided that if the Presidio de la Mesa del Tonatí seemed extinguishable, I should arrange it in accordance with the cited regulation by which there was ordered left there seven guards with 200 pesos each yearly and an officer with 14 men of the Catalonian Volunteer Company,[17] with only the military salary that they enjoyed, although to the commanding officer there be assigned an overage of 500 pesos annually in the form of a supplemental allowance.

17. The oft-encountered Catalonian Volunteers are treated in Joseph P. Sánchez, *Spanish Bluecoats: The Catalonian Volunteers in Northwestern New Spain, 1767–1810* (Albuquerque, 1990).

Orders Given as a Result of Decisions of That Meeting and Fortunate Results That They Produced

64. Before receiving government orders and desiring, motivated by my zeal, to forestall the damages that Chihuahua and its vicinity were suffering, I devoted myself to using actively the few troops that I had in carrying out personally and extensively the reconnaissance and examination of those lands. I ordered, dated 21 June [17]72, that the squads

of the presidios of Cerro Gordo and Guaxuquilla consist of 20 men each with its officer; that those of the city of Chihuahua, as well as those of the presidios of Julimes, San Buenaventura, Janos, and El Paso del Norte be comprised of 25 positions and their corresponding officer; and to all of them I indicated the lands, directions, and places that they ought to patrol and to oversee continually in the following manner:

Presidio de Cerro Gordo

65. The squad of this presidio patrolled downstream as far as Landebasua via San Bernardo, San Blas, Barraza, and from there to Los Reyes, from where it returned via the same places to the presidio.

Presidio de Guaxuquilla

66. The squad of this presidio patrolled leaving by way of Los Chupaderos to Carrisalillo; from there it took the road to Julimes or to the Ancón de Carros, from where it returned to the presidio following its own tracks.

Presidio de Julimes

67. The squad of this presidio patrolled leaving via El Paso de Cholomé to the Potrero de la Herran, as far as Hormigas, from where it returned to its presidio.

City of Chihuahua

68. The first squad patrolled via Palo Blanco to El Venado, Los Reyes, and El Barrigón, where it awaited the second [squad] which patrolled via Jesús María, La Cueva, Maxalca, Victorino, and El Potrero, following the base of the sierra as far as the Cañada de la Noria, which it searched continuing its route via the Laguna de San Martín as far as El Barrigón, where it joined with the first [squad]. After the officers gave each other testimony signed by two witnesses of having met at that place, they returned to the city via the same routes that they had taken.

Presidio de San Buenaventura

69. The squad of this presidio patrolled leaving via El Alamo to La Nariz, to Lo de Ruíz, via Lo de Velarde to the ford of the Río de Santa María, where it joined with the Janos squad, both going on to Las Salinas, from where they returned via the same places to the presidio.

Presidio de Janos

70. The squad of this presidio patrolled leaving via the Estancia de los Nogales to the ford of the Río de Santa María, where it met with the squad of San Buenaventura, and after both patrolled together as far as Las Salinas, it returned via the same places to its presidio.

Presidio de El Paso

71. The squad of this presidio patrolled via the Ojito de Samalayuca as far as Las Salinas, where it would either find or would await the squads of Janos and San Buenaventura, and after each of the three officers giving mutual certification in the indicated form of having met together at that place, they returned via the same places to their presidios.

72. It was arranged that all those squads should be out of the presidios for a period of 15 days engaged in patrolling and searching the lands that had been assigned to each one according to the previously expressed plan.

73. That for no reason should they change their destinations and routes, except only in the case of finding some trace of enemies entering or leaving, which if it were fresh or not very old, they should follow it and if they succeeded in overtaking them and find that the barbarians did not exceed 100 men, they should attack them without any delay, except if they might arrange to surprise them the following morning.

74. That if the number of barbarians should exceed 100 men, and because they are gathered together there might be time for joining with the squad or squads of the nearby presidios, opportune word should be passed, provided that in accordance with the itinerary assigned to each

squad, it would be possible to take into consideration the distances and places at which they could be found.

75. It was ordered that in such indispensable as well as difficult toil as this, the captains of the presidios and of the city of Chihuahua alternate with the lieutenants and ensigns, each going out for 15 days with their squads; and within 24 hours of one having arrived, the other should set out, for which purpose it ought to be ready and supplied, so that everything is always in continuous movement.

76. The captains and subordinate officers were bound by the obligation of keeping a detailed diary of the most important events during the 15 days and of the engagements that they succeeded in having with the enemies, as was many times necessary. In such a case they had to note accurately the place, the number of dead and wounded, and of captives that were taken of persons and horses, without forgetting the description of the losses that were suffered on our side, sending these documents each month to the high command in order by means of them to report to the government what has happened.

77. In the original diaries and reports that are found in the Archive of Chihuahua are clearly demonstrated the effects of these measures and the large number of horses and mules that it was possible to take from the Indians and return to their owners, in substantiation of which the treasurer of the expedition, who kept a detailed count, will testify. Meanwhile I can affirm to Your Lordship that up until then the citizens of Chihuahua and its vicinity had not been able to breathe easily from worry from the attacks made upon them by the many Indian *rancherías* inhabiting the nearby sierras, from which it was possible to remove them by dint of tireless persecution.

78. Later in two other Councils of War and of the Royal Treasury, it was decided to increase the Chihuahua company up to the number of 100 men; and another of 300 with whom I had talked; and to defray the expenses of the expedition, there was ordered sent out and there was applied to it the 100,000 pesos that were at Pitic in the province of Sonora.

79. I immediately devoted myself to recruitment of the 300 men, publishing a proclamation in Chihuahua and in the nearby towns so as to

achieve it more promptly. I sent officers to various places for the same purpose and by means of the [local] corregidor and other justices, I solicited the aid of the 25 Indians that it had been resolved to add to each company, with the 45 that already existed staying in Chihuahua.

80. Then, having recruited the number of men referred to, with satisfaction as regards their condition and aptitude for toil, I gave such orders as seemed to me proper for the purchase of horses and mules and I found myself in need of calling on the governor of the province to better insure success, without ceasing to make similar requests of other different people that in the future could make some ready, and it was at that time that the administrator of the Count of San Pedro de El Alamo supplied 472 horses in satisfaction of payment of his debt.

81. Next I sent to the government nominations for captains and other subordinate officers, and requested Don Manuel Antonio Escorza[18] as commissary and treasurer of the expedition, a person with the necessary qualities to carry out such a job and who was at that time completely separated from commerce.

82. I proceeded, in agreement with the intendant of Sonora, Pedro Corbalán, with the safe transport and receipt of the 100,000 pesos belonging to the Royal Treasury that was on hand in Pitic, providing escorts and other assistance. After that amount arrived in Chihuahua on 13 October, it was placed immediately in the hands of Treasurer Escorza; and there was also given to him for distribution the 10,000 pesos that the pay and daily allowances of the officers and troop of the Chihuahua company amounted to from 21 December of the past year of [17]71 when Don Bernardo de Gálvez turned over command until the day when the new captain of it, Don Francisco de la Borbolla,[19] took possession, accompanied at the same time by the monthly reviews of it that had been made by the corregidor.

83. I sent to the captains of the shifted presidios the written orders by which they were placed under my command. I sent to the governor of the province of Sonora the corresponding notice so that with knowledge of the operations that were planned against the barbarians and the times at which they would begin, he could carry out on his part what he should; and to those of Nueva Vizcaya and Coahuila the one that concerned carrying out the transfer of the presidios in their respective

18. In 1766 Escorza was *alcalde ordinario*, that is, regular alcalde of Chihuahua. From 1772 to 1779 he was treasurer of the Caja Real of Chihuahua. In 1775 he served as one of O'Conor's subordinates as commissary and treasurer of his expedition of that year.

19. Borbolla was captain of the second company of the O'Conor expedition.

provinces, which was what at the time seemed to me proper in fulfillment of the decisions of the junta.

84. It had contained therein the grounds and reasons upon which the Most Excellent Lord Marqués de Rubí argued for suppression of the four cited presidios, and since as regards that of Los Adaes, I advised the same when I was interim governor of the province of Texas, indicating its costly and useless existence, in which opinion Rear Admiral Don Antonio de Ulloa,[20] having reconnoitered its location, agreed with me, its suppression or retention was left to my decision, as well as that of the others that existed, according to what I considered logical.

85. This honorable confidence, and my desire of reciprocating it, obliged me to say in all fairness that the Presidio de los Adaes besides not contributing to the defense, could not serve offensively against the Apaches on the frontiers of Nueva Vizcaya and Coahuila, and even less for that of Texas to which it belongs, because of being located more than 300 leagues from the Río de San Antonio de Béxar, where the presidio of that name is situated, and where the Villa de San Fernando with its five missions is located, and from that of the Bahía del Espíritu Santo with another two [missions]. Besides there is the fact that the land is one of those on which the Lipan, Natages, and other Apache Indians have never set foot either in time of peace or in war because of the obstacle of distance, and because of many numerous barbarian nations that are their mortal enemies.

86. Practical knowledge of the land in which that presidio existed, without neighbors, towns, nor missions to support, which objective along with that of the reduction of barbarian nations is always the condition for establishing frontier [forts], made me think that way, adding that it has not been able to serve nor would it serve in the future for anything except to demarcate or separate the dominion of the King, our Sovereign, from that of His Most Christian Majesty [of France] as regards the province of Louisiana. But since that reason has ceased with the cession of it [Louisiana] and the transfer of its ownership to His Majesty, it did not seem to me that there was any other motive imaginable for the permanence of that presidio.

87. I also said that the one of Monterrey in the Kingdom of Nuevo León does not lead to nor is useful in blocking the barbarian Indians of the

20. Ulloa was a leading naval figure of his day. He teamed with Jorge Juan in an important scientific reconnaissance of South America, and was later made governor of Spanish Louisiana, in which position he was as much a failure as he had earlier been a success in exploration.

Apache nation, nor for offensive operations. I base my opinion on the fact that this presidio being not only a great distance from the enemy frontier, but also because of now being in the center of our settlements, has never used its troops against those nations, not even at the time of the fiercest warfare in the province of Texas, the governor remaining chiefly in the capital with the troop indicated in paragraph 61, and because of the lack of existence now of the fierce nation of the Tobosos who were those that previously attacked the province.

88. Moved by the same reasons, there was proposed the suppression in the province of Nayarit of the Presidio de la Mesa del Tonatí called San Francisco Xavier. Because of being in such a distant location and isolated from the provinces under attack, its forces would have been unable to serve them in any way nor give them help. I merely said that I was unable to find out if the one that existed served the original purpose of its creation.

89. I did point out affirmatively that it was in the midst of the sierra and in the center of many towns of Spaniards and of Indians and missions; that I knew that its individuals had revolted various times, attempting the expulsion of their ministers, and that from the year [17]54 until that of [17]63 they had waged war against the presidio and frontiers of the Pacific coast, making it necessary for the government to take proper measures for their punishment, and I conclude on the basis of not having enough information to judge with certainty, that I could not give a firm opinion whether or not its suppression would be fitting.

90. It did not turn out that way as regards the Presidio de San Antonio de Béxar, since being asked my opinion in the matter, I stated that it went without saying that the company should remain there with its personnel, which is composed of 41 men including the captain and the chaplain, and added to it that of San Agustín de Ahumada at Orcoquisac that served as a reinforcement for it by order of the government previous to the present one, and it consisted of a captain with 31 billets.

91. This reinforcement seemed to me sufficient for defense of that land, taking into consideration that the slight difference of 10 men was favorably supplemented by the residents of the Villa de San Fernando who would go out on campaign in emergencies, and by over 50 Indians who

I learned were kindly enlisted for such cases by the Father Ministers of the five nearby missions, armed and supplied with horses, arms, and whatever necessary.

92. There followed from such a course of action savings to the Royal Treasury of 3,800 pesos yearly, being the amount of the reduction of 10 billets, this figure at 380 pesos each, besides the possibility of one captain going out with the suitable troop, either to pursue the barbarians of the north if they continue their hostilities, or to aid in reduction of the infidels on the coast.

93. I was then occupied in carrying out these and other matters in my charge, when, among the many doubtful reports that I had of the opposition of the presidial captains to the important [and] proper project of the line of the sites as determined, I received the certain [report] that the governor of Coahuila was openly opposed to the relocation of presidios to the banks of the Río Grande del Norte that the royal junta had approved. But having expressed in my letter of 21 July [17]72 that which in my zeal for the service I deemed appropriate, what had been set forth was meaningless in opposition to the same royal junta that perhaps understood the causes from which said opposition sprang in this chief and in the other presidial captains. So I resolved that nothing be changed.

94. While these contentions were being questioned, in Chihuahua there began to arrive one after the other the horse herds that had been ordered purchased and the corresponding armament for the four mobile companies of the expedition, to whom everything was immediately distributed so that I could begin my operations.

95. With such help, I arranged these [operations] with the governors of the provinces of Sonora, [Nueva] Vizcaya, and Coahuila, and I decided on my departure to reconnoiter the confluence of the Río Grande del Norte, to which as a result they transferred the presidios of Cerro Gordo, Julimes, Monclova, Santa Rosa, and San Sabá, carrying out en route the dispossession of the many Indians that were found gathered together in the Bolsón de Mapimí, with the requirement that they cross to the opposite side of that river—a thing that they did either willingly or by

force of the punishment they imagined and in fact could fear because I never had greater hope of achieving it, according to the stipulation of my orders.

96. Meanwhile the province of Nueva Vizcaya was protected as much as possible since, in addition to the groups assigned to the protection of Chihuahua and its surrounding area, there were others that patrolled the land, all under the command of Lieutenant Colonel Manuel Muñoz, whose military spirit, bravery, and practical knowledge made me entrust it to him. And for the greater security of the lands to the east of that city, I ordered that a group of 20 men under an officer of the Presidio de Guaxuquilla be posted in the place called Ancón de Carros, and I ordered that an equal number be maintained in the vicinity of the Pueblo de San Gerónimo, without any other that could patrol the entrances of the place called La Noria and the Cañada del Fresno, all places through which the Indians were accustomed to make their frequent incursions.

97. Having taken these measures, I left on the indicated expedition accompanied by the first, third, and fourth mobile companies, and after tedious and laborious maneuvers I not only achieved the aforementioned dispossession, but also made evident to the barbarians what the arms of the King were like when there were serious attempts to make them glorious, although in hands as inferior as mine, since in measures of the Most High, He avails Himself of any instrument.

98. About this time the new presidio regulations [21] with the instructions drawn up by the government arrived in my hands, and according to one and the other, I marked out for the time being the land that the presidios of Monclova and Santa Rosa should occupy prior to suitable examination. Leaving their respective companies to the work on their new buildings, with proper help so as not to impede progress, I continued my march along the entire river mentioned, pointing out the places where the presidios of San Antonio Bucareli, San Sabá, San Carlos, and that of the Junta de los Ríos currently occupy on the line, and I returned to Chihuahua with no greater result in the several skirmishes that I had with the barbarians than the loss of one soldier [of the third company] who died of his wounds.

21. A bilingual edition of the royal presidial regulations is presented in Sidney B. Brinckerhoff and Odie B. Faulk, *Lancers for the King* (Phoenix, 1965).

99. Eight days after my arrival in Chihuahua, it was necessary to make an inspection review and to put in order the companies that would garrison the three presidios then named Cerro Gordo, Guaxuquilla, and Julimes. After having carried it out in the months of July and August of that year of [17]73 with the detail that the documents sent to this superior government substantiate, I returned to the city in order to provide myself with the necessary food supplies for the subsequent operations.

100. Having made suitable preparations and so that enemy invasion to the interior of the province not be carried out, I ordered the garrisoning of the entire frontier from the Sierra de Carretas to El Ojo Caliente with squads of the third and fourth mobile companies of the expedition, and that the first company enter from the south to reconnoiter the Bolsón de Mapimí, with the obligation of meeting me at the Río Grande del Norte at the place called San Carlos. I assigned the second [company] for the defense of the city of Chihuahua and its environs, with orders and instructions to the officers named for command of the squads of what they should do in their respective sectors to guard the frontier. I left Chihuahua early in the month of October of [17]73 with the two companies of dragoons of Spain and of Mexico that were still serving there; and directing my march to the Presidio de Julimes, I ordered that at it there join with me those removed from Cerro Gordo and Guaxuquilla with their families and other things necessary for their establishment on the Río Grande del Norte.

101. I continued my march with all this cumbersome train as far as the cited river, and after leaving each of those presidios in their respective lands, I returned with the two dragoon companies to the junction of the Río del Norte and the Conchos [La Junta]; and on the second day after my arrival the sentinel sighted a cloud of dust that was coming along the entire river. It was, as I deduced, the company of Don Domingo Díaz that was to incorporate with me, which officer informed me that in the entire Bolsón de Mapimí not a trace of Indians had been found since the last reconnaissance that I made of those lands.

102. Having successfully completed the preceding movements and desirous of finding a way that the new presidios could work on the rough buildings of their compounds without being bothered by enemies, I

deduced that the most certain way to achieve it would be by punishment of them in their own *rancherías*. For that purpose I therefore set out from the Presidio de la Junta de los Ríos, and crossing the Río Grande del Norte at the beginning of November of the year [17]73, accompanied by the two dragoon companies and the first [company] of the expedition, with the proper precautions I continued my march toward the Río Colorado until the 26th day of that month when the squads that were patrolling to the right and to the left informed me of having found many tracks that entered the dense Sierra del Mogano.[22]

103. As it was then night, I ordered my troops to encamp at the spring that is located at the slope of the sierra in order to rest from the fatigue they had suffered during the quick marches that it had been necessary to make, particularly during the last two days when we traveled without stopping either by day or by night in order to overtake the Indians whom we supposed were fleeing from us. I took advantage of the existing moonlight and set out with 12 men to scout the sierra, the ruggedness of which did not allow us to find the ground or place occupied by the enemy, although from them and through signs made by their spies, we were led to understand that they were there. At about midnight I returned to camp and, preparing everything needed to attack them at daybreak of the following day, the 27th of November, I marched with my troop for the sierra; and entering by one of its canyons and on the track of the enemy at a distance of a league and in the most rugged part of it, more than 600 Indians attacked me with vigor and bravery. But High Providence on which everything depends granted me the most complete victory over them without having on our side any other mishaps than two soldiers who came out slightly wounded, to which glorious battle must constantly be attributed the completion of the buildings of the eastern presidios, for since then the enemy has not been seen for a long time.[23]

104. After this campaign I retired to the Presidio de las Juntas on 30 December from where I departed on the 9th to reconnoiter, arrange, and relocate the western presidios, because of the urgency of doing so. Continuing my march with 50 men, relatively exposed due to their small number and the rigorous cold of the winter months, I managed at the expense of infinite trouble to mark out the land where the presidios of El Príncipe, San Elezeario, San Fernando de El Carrizal, San Buenaven-

22. The site of O'Conor's great victory over the Apaches, probably the Natages, was in West Texas or in southern New Mexico. When the place name Mogano is mentioned in documents of that period it is usually located in the vicinity of the Sierra de Guadalupe and the Sierra del Diablo. However, the translators and editors of O'Conor's report of 30 January 1776 equate the Sierra del Mogano with the Davis Mountains, somewhat farther southeast.

23. According to Navarro García, *Don José de Gálvez*, p. 233, during his third expedition O'Conor had come across a large group of Apaches at the mouth of the Sierra de Mogano. On 27 November 1773, after commending his party to María Inmaculada, the attack took place in which O'Conor defeated more than 500 enemies, chasing them four leagues and killing 40. Navarro cites as his source O'Conor's diary in the Archivo General de Indias, Guadalajara 513.

tura, and Janos were to be located, and passing review of their respective companies, I relocated them to the lands where they are today.

105. Having returned to Chihuahua, I received a government order for my transfer to the province of Coahuila. I did so on 27 March 1774 after giving orders that I considered proper for defense, and I did the same in Coahuila, entrusting compliance of them to the governor, Don Jacobo de Ugarte y Loyola.[24]

106. This trip gave me opportunity to reexamine the line and to inspect the status of the rude buildings of the presidios, being those in which their respective companies were found. I continued in that important occupation until the end of November of that same year, at which time I ordered a sortie for the purpose of punishing the barbarians whom I learned were gathered together in some mountains 60 leagues northwest of the Presidio de Janos, from where they emerged to disturb the frontier with their pillage.

107. Fortunately having achieved their punishment and capture, I ordered them taken to the Presidio de El Carrizal to thus avoid all risk. On 15 January I moved to El Paso del Norte for the purpose of forming the militia companies called for in the ordinance. As a result of this operation, Your Lordship will find in that pueblo four [companies], each of 53 men including the officers.

108. Having transacted this business, I returned to the Presidio de El Carrizal where I had usually resided during the brief periods that the cares of command permitted me to do so. There I formalized the plan of operations for the general campaign that I had proposed and that when sent to the government had won its approval, and I began to carry it out.

109. For this purpose I left Carrizal for Chihuahua on 30 March. I gave appropriate orders for the collection of food. I got rid of the group of captive Indians taken prisoner during my sorties, sending them to this capital in the charge of Dragoon Captain Manuel Pardo. With approval of that superior government, I drew up the regulation by which the four mobile companies are governed. Determined to go on to Sonora in order to return in time to carry out the campaign, I moved to that province

24. Jacobo Ugarte y Loyola must have a near record for longevity in the service, some 62 years from cadet to field marshal. As a colonel he was governor of Coahuila. In 1777 he became governor of Sonora, followed by the governorship of Puebla. Next he was commandant of the Provincias Internas del Occidente, after the division of that command. Finally he was commanding general of Nueva Galicia and president of the Royal Audiencia that had its seat there, as well as being governor and intendant of the province.

on 22 May. In it I reviewed and put in order the presidial companies. I inspected the lands on which the four presidios to be moved, of Fronteras, Terrenate, Tubac, and Santa Gertrudis del Altar, would be located. I drew up the general report of my observations in that province and with the prior approval of the government, I decided on the relocation of the first to the valley of San Bernardino; the second to the place called Santa Cruz; the third to that of San Agustín del Tuquison [Tucson]; and the fourth to that of Escomac. Afterward I returned to the Nueva Vizcaya frontier to prepare things concerning the aforementioned general campaign.

110. On 13 September, I arrived without incident at the Presidio de San Buenaventura; and with no more than six days rest, I carried out my new sortie, achieving fortunately the result that I had proposed of punishing and teaching a lesson to the barbarians, among which results was the successful reduction of the Navajo Apaches to their former towns from which they had attacked the two provinces of Nueva Vizcaya and New Mexico.

111. By the appended status reports numbered first, second, and third, Your Lordship will learn of the number of presidios by province of which the new line is formed from sea to sea; of the final completion of its provisional buildings except for some internal works that are lacking at those of Monclova and Santa Rosa, and those of the three in the province of Sonora — Santa Cruz, San Agustín del Tuquison, and Santa Gertrudis del Altar — although it is probable that those will be finished in a short time as a result of the help of the Indians of the two missions of San Xavier del Wac [Bac] and San Agustín; and of [the fact] that the two of Bahía del Espíritu Santo and San Juan Bautista del Río Grande have not been moved from their old lands because both are on line and thus called for in the Royal Instruction.

112. In those documents Your Lordship will also see the effective force of the presidios; that of the mobile corps of the expedition and of the militia of the pueblo of El Paso; the position of the cavalry and mule herd, and the annual cost to the King of the entire line, with a statement on salaries in which those of the inspector of presidios and his two assistants is included.

113. All the presidial troop is of superior quality in size and strength, of valor and perseverance for the hardship of its difficult purpose, very skillful in riding horseback and in the useful and adaptable maneuvers for the type of war they wage. In the many actions of which I have been witness, they have demonstrated their training in handling of arms, in their love of the service and in their painstaking desire to punish the barbarians, for which they have not spared risks nor hardships. Rather to the contrary, they have willingly undergone hunger, thirst, and other inconveniences that war continually produces when it is waged in such extended and unpopulated lands as those which Your Lordship is going to govern.

114. When I relinquished command each soldier had on hand the seven horses and a mule that the ordinance indicates for them. The uniform that the troop uses is identical in all the provinces and consists of a short jacket of woolen cloth or blue cloth with a small edging and red collar, gilt buttons, blue woolen trousers, a cloth cape of the same color, a cartridge pouch, jacket, and bandoleer of chamois leather on which there is embroidered the name of the presidio, a black neckerchief, hat, shoes, and leggings; and all was in good condition when I left the frontier.

115. The armament consisted of a broadsword of the size and shape that the other army cavalry use, a lance, a shield, a shotgun and pistols, of the sort sent by order of the King to these frontiers for use in its presidios; the proper spares existed and their full value was discounted in favor of the Royal Treasury by the royal officers of San Luis Potosí, Real de los Alamos, and the treasurer of the city of Chihuahua.

116. In the storehouse of each of the presidios there was found to exist a resupply of powder equivalent to eight pounds per individual billet, and under the protection of two keys of which the captain had one and the supply officer had the other.

117. The riding gear includes a cowboy saddle with the corresponding accoutrements called knapsack, cuirass, arms, pads, and wooden stirrups; and all was in good condition at the time of my departure.

118. In the cash box of the 10-peso allowance per billet, there was found that corresponding to the time from when I placed the companies on

the new footing of the ordinances until December of the previous year (with the exception of those of the presidios of Monclova, Santa Rosa, and El Príncipe whose captains have not observed the articles of the Royal Instruction), and the accounts presented of the common expenses that have been offered were legal, the documents of which were deposited in the same [boxes] for proof: and for payment due of 100 pesos per billet that each soldier should have in savings for the purposes expressed in Article 2, Title 5 of the Royal Instruction, the retention of 20 pesos yearly for each has been made, which fund was deposited in cash boxes with three keys, and of these one is in the hands of each of the company officers.

119. With the formation of the line of presidios, free communication is open between the provinces of Texas, Coahuila, [Nueva] Vizcaya, Sonora, and New Mexico; and in each presidio the routine that they should observe for daily service and for the patrols that the squads must continually make is established; how there should be formalized the adjustment of pay, status of debits and credits of each company; chits for the liquidation of a soldier's private account and the general one of the supply officer and for the extension of enlistments of the recruits that in the future should be done in the reviews and diaries of their operations that must be sent in monthly; lists of the effective force of their respective companies; condition of uniforms, arms, and saddles; the system that should be maintained for the dispatch of the monthly mail, with the other documents and orders that I issued and that lead to the most correct, just management of the presidial companies; the method by which these should carry out their campaigns; and an instructive report of the sierras, canyons, watering places, and lands that the enemies normally inhabit, the knowledge of which the presidial troops in general lacked until now.

120. All those advancements have been carried out at the cost of great vigilance and of a tireless zeal for the service, with no chance that the frontier would be further invaded, and nobody as much as I has known how much the chief's presence is worth everywhere. In all actions that I had with the barbarians I fortunately came out victorious, reestablishing the honor of the King's arms, which was in decay when I took command of those provinces.

121. To achieve this, I have not spared time, fatigue, nor discomfort, and if Your Lordship stops to consider that in the short time of a little over five years I have traveled through unknown places, through unknown mountains and canyons, and via unknown forests and rivers, traveling nearly 4,000 leagues during which I myself have moved the presidios of Sonora and [Nueva] Vizcaya; reviewing them and readying their companies and dislodging enemies from the vast territory that they occupied over a distance of 700 leagues from east to west and 200 from north to south, you will perceive the difference that there is in the state of the frontier compared to that of the year [17]71. At that time the barbarians were full of insolence and pride due to the advantages that they gained at every turn and a small number of them attacked our force which was twice their size, as is evident from various examples. Today completely the contrary happens, and as long as the patrols that I ordered are continued and there is found among the officers the constancy that they are becoming used to, and they do not let themselves be taken by surprise, as has occasionally been seen, the barbarians will live restrained, depending on how many of those chastised are left.

122. Many actions could be cited to substantiate this contention, but since Your Lordship has in the Archive of Chihuahua documents very corroborative of them, it will be sufficient that I cite the one that the gallant and experienced officer Narciso Tapia[25] had with the bold Indians of the west in the place of the Estancia de Becerra that gave so much glory to the arms of the monarch, and the one that I personally commanded at the Caxón del Mogano, from which the new line of presidios resulted, which would have been carried out with great difficulty had not the barbarians been overcome by fear as a result of the setback they received.

123. Although under the new regulation the two presidios of San Miguel de Horcasitas and San Carlos de Buenavista in Sonora are ordered extinguished, the government did not want to do anything new until I should go to the province and review those to be removed. Before this event, they had deliberated the transfer of those two to the banks of the Colorado and Gila rivers, and I thought the same, provided some force be left in the two places they [now] occupy, for which purpose and until settlement of the Seri and Yaqui Indians, I asked that the mobile company be substituted in their place.

25. Narciso Tapia, hero of the battle at the Estancia de Becerra, near Janos, served as second ensign of O'Conor's third company.

124. By moving the two referred to presidios to the rivers indicated, as the King has approved, the attainment of favorable progress is possible among the many nations that have been recently explored by the Father Missionary Fray Francisco Garcés[26] between the province of Moqui and the new acquisitions in California, or at least it will keep clear the road between them that Lieutenant Colonel Juan Bautista de Anza[27] opened, provided the Yumas and other nations who have just declared themselves as friends remain firm in their intention.

125. In the Archive of Chihuahua Your Lordship will find the original provisions concerning the method of making payments to the troop, providing powder to them, and by whom, as well as what has been directed about repayment of the cost of armament that should be distributed to the soldiers when they need it.

126. Almost all the presidios have the supply of arms that the Royal Ordinance stipulates, but since this is not so with the mobile corps of the expedition upon whom the principal defense of the frontiers depend, it will be advisable, so that this troop not lack this such indispensable assistance for its subsequent operations, that it be provided with those necessary in accordance with its effective force.

127. The rules that by their constitution the presidial troops observe are to guard their presidio and cavalry; to provide sufficient guards for the collection and transport of foodstuffs and goods that their garrisons need; to patrol the nearby lands; to aid reciprocally the groups assigned to it; and to make the campaigns that are directed in accordance with the orders of the chief.

128. Those of the mobile corps are also employed in the gathering and transport of foodstuffs and supplies that their subsistence requires, with their squads continually occupied in patrolling all the vast territory that stretches from the Sierra de Carretas which is to the west of the Presidio de Janos, to as far as that of San Antonio Bucareli, the first one in Coahuila, and from the campsite called Ancón de Carros as far as the old Presidio de El Gallo, and the area surrounding Chihuahua, without thereby omitting carrying out their respective campaigns.

26. Franciscan Father Francisco Hermenegildo Garcés was born in Morata del Conde in Aragón. As a young priest he went to the New World. He served in Sonora, and in exploration of the far frontiers beyond. He is best known for his explorations to California and throughout much of Arizona, and for his martyr's death at the crossing of the Colorado River on 17 July 1781 in what has been called the Yuma Massacre.

27. Juan Bautista de Anza was the son and grandson of frontier military officers. He is best known for his opening the overland trail from Sonora to California in 1774 and 1775. He later became governor of New Mexico.

129. Despite these measures that my knowledge and experience have made me believe opportune, it is impossible to prevent completely the plundering and robberies that the barbarians carry out in the interior of the province, because commonly they are usually small groups that succeed in entering without being seen along the same line of presidios.

130. It has been done that way in my time, and may be learned by practice in the future, if one bears in mind the cunning with which some hostile Indians usually invade. Nevertheless, if one compares the invasions and damages of recent times with those that the barbarians committed before the formation of the mobile corps and the establishment of the new plan, the advantages attained will be clearly seen, since in addition to the fact that deaths and robberies have not been so frequent, they have not experienced the abandonment of places, estates, nor some ranches which were daily noted. Rather, to the contrary, they are seen to have been repopulated from then on, as is evident by decrees, many that had been uninhabited; and above all the very city of Chihuahua is an exceptional witness that will be able to testify concerning the tranquillity that it enjoys with restitution made in my time of more than 7,000 animals of those they have been able to take away from the Indians. This being noted, and that such happy consequences relate directly to the well-being of the frontier in general, I continue on by saying what concerns the troop especially and the consequences that ensue from it to the service.

Beneficial Effects That the New Plan Has Produced

131. According to the old presidio plan, and in proportion to the distances that they were from this court [Mexico City], its individuals had different salaries. Some 420 pesos; others 400, and some 380, whose income was supplied to them by their respective captains in merchandise without finding an example of having given out a peso in cash, for lack of which and its circulation, it resulted that there did not exist towns, nor any appreciable commerce on the frontier, since it is clear

that the captains, for the purpose of increasing their wealth, prevented under great penalty the entrance to their presidios of traders and other people whom they believed might be prejudicial.

132. The soldier who in those days enjoyed the greatest salary did not actually touch a full 100 pesos a year according to the accounts in the cash book that both the Marqués de Rubí and I paid off several times.

133. From such a deceitful practice there followed the obligation of 400 and more pesos to the soldier at the end of the year, from which resulted his inaction even in the case of enemy invasion, as has happened many times, since the captain fearing that with the death of the soldier he would doubtless lose that person's obligation, he never permitted the troops to leave the presidio to restrain the enemies in their hostilities. Moreover, there coincided many other considerations of abuses and excesses that were borne in mind in the formation of the Royal Regulation of 10 September 1772.

134. By its fortunate establishment, they have been able to liberate the troop from its ancient oppression, since although by it the soldier does not receive more than 290 pesos salary per year and 10 of gratuity, he obtains the very great advantage of receiving from the hands to the supply officer merchandise at prime cost, as well as 2-1/2 reales daily which is given in cash in the presence of all the company, and finally they are given the balance that some frequently have of 30, 40, 60, 80, or even 100 pesos with the supply officer at the end of the year. Most worthwhile of all is the liberty that they enjoy of being able to buy merchandise wherever it is cheapest.

135. From this reasonable measure, one not only infers the equity with which the soldier must be treated, but also that with the circulation of cash in those provinces, there is gained the gathering together of many people, with some of them settling there, and the former aptly serving, gloriously risking his life whenever the occasion presents itself, as has been done repeatedly, without the captain having misgivings that he might lose some profit with the soldier's death.

136. Since the utility of so many points contained in the Royal Instruction is known, in my opinion its fulfillment must be carefully observed,

without permitting in such an important matter that there ever be any deviation because of the most fatal consequences that could be produced by any innovation whatsoever that might be made.

137. Perhaps there might be persons who propose under the pretext of utility establishing on the frontier one, two, or three trading houses, assuming the convenience that it will be for the supply officers to provide themselves there with the necessary provisions for the subsistence of their respective presidios. But if such were carried out, it would be to destroy entirely the pious, wise, and useful rules that the Royal Instruction lays down for the management of funds.

138. If the misfortune of the Provincias Internas should reach such a point, consequently monopolizing among one, two, or three persons something more than a half million pesos that annually circulate among its people, there will then be seen, and with anguish, not only the general displeasure of the troop but also the total depopulation of those lands and the repeated complaints of the merchants, as those who are most directly injured.

139. To avoid such dire results, there is no surer way than that provided in the Royal Instruction, requiring that everywhere its fulfillment be observed and with the exactness that it had been done in my time, since in not doing it that way, according to my understanding, it will cut off the progress for which it is directed and ruin the provinces instead of making them rich, as the King desires and as suits the well-being of his crown.

Status of the Indians Who Attack the Frontier

140. The Apaches who terrify the provinces of Sonora and Nueva Vizcaya are known by the names Chiricagui, Gileños, Mimbreños, Mescaleros, Faraones, the *rancherías* of Pascual, that of Ligero, that of

Alonso, that of Chief Bigotes, and the Natagé. The first three in the Apache language are called Sigilandé, Setozende, Chiguende, and the rest Zetozende, Selcotisanende, Culcahende, Cachuguinde, Yncagende, Sigilande, and Zetozende.

141. The first three nations mentioned normally reside in the extended and rough sierras of Chiricagui, Gila, Mimbres, La Florida, Cerro Gordo, Sangre de Christo, Corral de San Agustín, Capulin, Corral de Piedra, Sierra Obscura, the Blanca, that of Sacramento, the Organos, Petaca, Sierra de los Ladrones, that of La Magdalena, that of Enmedio, the Ojo de Abeitia, Sierra de la Hacha, Las Espuelas, La Mogina, La Boca, Corral de Quintero, Mesas de Robledo, sierras of El Paso del Norte, Cerro Hueco, San Nicolás, and various others that are located beyond the presidios of Sonora, and the three in the west of [Nueva] Vizcaya—Janos, San Buenaventura, and San Fernando de El Carrizal—and the rest of the nations cover all the land found on the other side of the Río Grande del Norte as far as the Colorado, taking refuge in the sierras that run from west to east, called the Guadalupe, Mogano, Sierra Nevada, Chanate, that of Cornudo, that of El Ayre, Cola del Aguila, Sierra del Diablo, and its chain as far as the Río San Pedro, from where those Indians usually emerge to commit their hostilities both in the province of Nueva Vizcaya and in Coahuila as well, so that only the Natagé is little inclined to the sierras, for which reason they gather together most of the time on the banks of the Río Colorado and places called Los Arenales and [Los] Pozos.

Warfare That They Are Accustomed to Wage

142. According to the seasons of the year, those barbarians inhabit those places that offer the best advantages for their support and for pasture for their horse herds, but always in the interior, yet hidden and protected by the sierras, motivated by the security for their wives and chil-

dren and for their crops of corn and other products, but without the need of maintaining and guarding these lands, because of having the same thing in any other place.

143. The armed men normally travel away from their rancherias, and almost unceasingly into our lands, with no other purpose than that of robbery and creating all the damage they can.

144. The dress of the men is composed of a feather band, and some chamois or buffalo skins; their food is whatever the land taken by their arms offers, eating all kinds of animals, particularly horses and mules and various plants and roots.

145. Their arms are the pike or lance and a bow and arrows; their blanket, which among us is the shield or buckler, and some buckskin. They have some firearms that they acquired in barter with the Vidais Indians[28] who reside near Louisiana and an abundance of horses, both because of the many they have stolen as well as those they raise, since these serve them as food.

28. Modern spelling is Bidais for these natives who lived on the lower portion of the middle fork of the Trinity River in Texas.

146. They always travel in various squads wandering over our lands and roads. Being knowledgeable of the land, they occupy the places that are most advantageous to them. They likewise prepare their attacks, but in such a way that they have never done so, nor ever will do so, when our numbers are equal to theirs, but rather with such obvious superiority that their victory is certain; and since they are not required to defend themselves, nor maintain any place, spot, or town, they wait for when their number is incomparably greater, and flee when they feel themselves to be few.

147. From all of which it is gathered that this is a kind of enemy that in order to keep up war for many years does not need the same measures as all civilized people, such as funds, and subsidies for pay, arms, munitions, foodstuffs and supplies, mule trains for transportation and cartage, enlistment of men, storage of grain, and many other indispensable preparations for the purpose, since all are veteran soldiers and even nurtured in warfare, paid, armed, and supplied at all times, everywhere, and on all occasions, without any other employment, occupa-

tion, or trade necessary for their support, nor for that of their wives and children.

148. Last year, 1773, and in total conformity with the prudent warnings of this superior government, peace was made with the Lipan Indians and, according to my understanding, they have since then become quiet, with the exception of a few of them who usually join with the Mescaleros to commit their robberies and murders.

149. Although the entire nation of these Lipan Indians has tried to remain constant in their promised faithfulness, it does not seem proper that, for the excesses committed by some of its individuals, the punishment of all has been urged, which in such a case does not present just a few problems, and in truth can produce most bitter consequences.

150. Once this is agreed to, I am of the opinion that these Indians should be treated in the same way as the King orders in Article 6, Title 10 of the Royal Instruction of 10 September [17]72, and that there is maintained with them the best treatment and friendship, tolerating in them some mistakes or slight excesses and trying to induce them by good example and persuasion to admit missionaries and that they submit to the King's rule.

151. If occasionally they (as is customary) commit the robbery of horses or other excesses that it is not proper to overlook, and when demanded they do not make restitution, it can be required of them by force, doing them the least possible harm so as not to offend the spirit of the entire nation, because of the hope that there now is that in time and in dealing with the Spaniards their desired reduction to missions or pueblos can be achieved.

152. Leaving for later treatment the province of Texas which is located more than a degree beyond our line, and the vast warlike nations of the north that surround it, I will pass on to give an idea of defensive and offensive war that, according to what I think, should be made on the Apaches that commit hostilities on the provinces of Sonora, Nueva Vizcaya, New Mexico, and Coahuila, both to prevent plundering by those enemies as well as to subject them to royal authority.

153. For the success of such an important object there is located on the frontier a string of presidios that extends 500 leagues a little more or less from the Presidio de la Bahía del Espíritu Santo as far as that of Santa Gertrudis del Altar, the mobile corps of the expedition, and two detachments of dragoons that by royal order do their duty there.

154. Since defensive war has as its object the prevention of entry of the enemy into the interior of the provinces; pursuit and punishment of those who by cunning can invade past our presidios, thereby facilitating the tranquillity of the residents of those lands, the business of their commerce, safety of the royal highways, and security of the rural estates; the most certain means of achieving it will always be the vigilance of the squads that are assigned to their respective lands, to cover and patrol daily the lands in the places that lie between one presidio and the other in the way that has been done up to now, mutually aiding each other, since as a result of the route assigned to each one, it will be easy for them to know the place or places where they can be found, and if my rules may be adaptable, I will describe to Your Lordship those I devised for the greatest security of the frontier.

155. The presidial squads and the mobile corps of the expedition must be composed of the number of men and officers that the commander in chief may consider appropriate to assign for each one, and mindful of the number of the enemy.

Presidio de Santa Gertrudis del Altar

156. The squad of this presidio should patrol as far as the abandoned mission of Sonoita and from there to the new presidio of San Agustín del Tuquison, from where it will return via the same places to its presidio.

San Agustín del Tuquison

157. That of this presidio will patrol leaving by way of the Mission of San Xavier del Wac [Bac] to the Ojito de Agua, having on its right the large sierra of Santa Rita and on its left that of Santa Catarina, following its route via the banks of the Río San Pedro, Parage de Tres Alamos,

as far as the Presidio de Santa Cruz, from where it will return over its own track to its presidio.

Presidio de Santa Cruz

158. The squad of this presidio will patrol leaving via El Vado de las Palominas to La Soledad, and from there over flat lands and without mountains or hills of which there are none, and following the well-known Sierra de Chiricagui, it will arrive at the Presidio de San Bernardino, from which it will return to its presidio over the same route that it took.

Presidio de San Bernardino

159. That of this presidio will patrol leaving via La Tinaja, the difficult Cañada de Guadalupe, over the Llano de San Luis, leaving to its right the Sierra de Enmedio, via La Palotada as far as the Presidio de Janos, from where it will march to its presidio over the same trail.

Presidio de Janos

160. The squad of this presidio will patrol to the Estancia de Becerra, Puerto de los Nogales, and leaving to its right the Sierra de la Escondida, it will arrive at the Presidio de San Buenaventura, from which it will return over the same route to its presidio.

Presidio de San Buenaventura

161. That of this presidio will patrol leaving by way of the Puerto de Las Bazas, Ojo de Santo Domingo, as far as the Presidio de El Carrizal, from where it will make its return to its presidio by way of the same places.

San Fernando de El Carrizal

162. That of this presidio will patrol leaving via the Laguna de Patos to the Ojo de León, and leaving on its left hand the Sierra de la Ranchería, it will arrive at the Presidio de San Elezeario, and from here it will return to its presidio via the same route.

Presidio de San Elezeario

163. The squad of this presidio will patrol to the Ojos Calientes, Caxón Chico, and along the banks of the Río Grande del Norte it will continue its march as far as the Presidio de El Príncipe, from where it will be able to return to its presidio.

Presidio de El Príncipe

164. That of this presidio must patrol along the banks of the Río Grande del Norte as far as that of the Junta de los Ríos, from where it will return for its presidio over the same track.

Presidio de la Junta de Los Ríos

165. That of this presidio will patrol leaving via Los Puliques to the Ojo de Agua de San Joseph, to that of La Consolación, to that of San Carlos as far as the presidio of that name, from where it will return by way of the same places to its own.

Presidio de San Carlos

166. The squad of this presidio will patrol to the Arroyo de El Alamo, Parage de la Zabeneta, to that of Las Peñitas, leaving on its left the Sierra de los Chizos, and on arriving at the Presidio de San Sabá, it will return to its own via the same route.

Presidio de San Sabá

167. That of this presidio will patrol along the exit of the canyon to the Aguage de la Salada, Las Torresitas, Las Cruces, or the Cuesta de los Capitanes, Parage de las Cabras, until it arrives at the Presidio de San Antonio Bucareli de la Bavia, returning from here to theirs over the same track.

Presidio de San Antonio Bucareli

168. That of this presidio will patrol to Las Rocitas de San Juan, the Sierra del Pino, and crossing this it will go along the banks of the Río Grande del Norte as far as the Presidio de Santa Rosa at the place called

Agua Verde, reconnoitering El Paso de Rabago, and the *bolsón* that is formed between the Río Grande del Norte and said Sierra del Pino; and examining all this land with the greatest care, it will return via the same places to its presidio.

Presidio de Santa Rosa

169. The squad of this presidio will patrol via the banks of the Río Grande del Norte to the ford of Santa Theresa, to that of San Antonio, to the junction of the Río Grande del Norte and the Río San Diego, as far as the Presidio de la Monclova, from where it will return over the same track to its own [presidio].

Presidio de la Monclova

170. That of this presidio will patrol along the banks of the Río Grande del Norte as far as to where the Río Escondido joins with it, and from there to the Presidio de San Juan Bautista, returning by the same route to its presidio.

Presidio de San Juan Bautista

171. The squad of this presidio will patrol crossing the Río Grande del Norte as far as the Nueces, where it will join with that of the Presidio de San Antonio de Béxar, and after the officers give each other a receipt, it will return via the same road to its presidio.

Presidio de San Antonio de Béxar

172. That of this presidio will patrol leaving to the Parage del Atascoso, to the Río de Medina, until arriving at the Nueces where it will join with the squad of the Presidio de San Juan Bautista, and after the officers mutually give each other a receipt of having met at that river of Las Nueces, it will return via the same places to its presidio.

Detachment of the Arroyo de Cíbolo[29]

173. The squad of this detachment will leave to the east patrolling as far as the Parage de las Tetillas, where it will meet that of the Presidio de

29. According to Elizabeth A. H. John, *Storms Brewed in Other Men's Worlds* (College Station, 1975), p. 198, the post was located on Cíbolo Creek at the Tawakoni Crossing about 45 miles southeast of San Antonio. A small fortification was built there in 1771.

la Bahía del Espíritu Santo, and after the officers mutually give certification of having met together at that place, it will march on its own tracks to its detachment.

Presidio de la Bahía del Espíritu Santo

174. The squad of this presidio will patrol leaving via Las Garcitas to the Arroyo del Arrastradero to Las Tetillas, where it will join the squad from the detachment of the Arroyo del Cíbolo, and after the officers mutually give certification of having been in that place, it will return on the same track to its presidio.

175. Each and every one of the squads mentioned must be out of their presidios for a period of 15 days, employed in patrolling and searching the lands that are assigned to each.

176. It will be fitting to warn them that for no reason are they to vary from those routes or places, except only in the case of finding some trace of the enemy entering or leaving, which if it be fresh or not very old, they should follow it and if they succeed in overtaking them and by investigating they find that they do not exceed 100 men, they will attack without any delay, except if they can arrange to surprise them the following morning.

177. If the number of barbarians should exceed 100 men, and because they are gathered together there is time for joining with the squad or squads of the nearby presidios, appropriate word will be given, provided that in accordance with the itinerary assigned to each squad it will be possible to take into consideration the distance and places where they might be found.

178. In this so indispensable as well as praiseworthy toil, the captains should alternate with the lieutenants and ensigns so that each one goes out 15 days with his squad. Within 24 hours of one having arrived, the other will set out, which must be ready and provisioned for this purpose, so that it is always evident that all are in continual movement.

179. The captains and subalterns will keep as has already been said an accurate diary of the most important events during their 15 days, and

of the engagements that they succeed in having with the enemies, as will many times be necessary, and in this case they ought to note the place, the number of dead and wounded, if it can be done; and the persons, horses, and mules that they take from them; and likewise the dead and wounded, and any other losses whatsoever on our side; with the captains sending it each month to the high command, so that the commander in chief is fully informed of everything that may have occurred, both favorable as well as unfavorable.

180. The squads of the mobile corps of the expedition can occupy the same lands that are indicated from the Presidio de Fronteras to that of San Antonio Bucareli de la Bavia, making their patrols in the same way as is stipulated for the presidio troops.

181. In the city of Chihuahua, there has always been maintained a company for its defense and that of its surroundings.

182. Another [company] of the mobile corps is assigned to cover all the land that extends as far as the place called Ancón de Carros, including as far as the old Presidio de El Gallo, with the intention of stopping the robberies and deaths committed by the barbarians who enter via the Bolsón de Mapimí to the vicinity of El Parral, the valley of San Bartolomé, Real del Oro, Hacienda de la Zarca, and everything in that direction.

183. With these measures, which are those that I ordered to be observed, not only will the garrisoning of the frontier be achieved, our squads covering daily the 500 leagues, more or less, that there are from the Presidio de la Bahía del Espíritu Santo to as far as that of Santa Gertrudis del Altar, but also the inhabitants of [Nueva] Vizcaya will be freed from the continual attacks that they used to suffer.

184. It will be no less important that with the squads they reconnoiter frequently the sierras that are found behind our line of presidios to prevent the enemies fortifying themselves in them, who usually enter there with such subtlety that the squads assigned to patrol those lands many times do not notice them until after they have already committed damage in the interior of the province.

185. So that the reconnaissance be made with the promptness and knowledge that is proper, I will name here the sierras and places where refuge is usually taken by the Indians that enter along our line, and these are the following: Pastor de la Mula, El Barrigón, Agua Nueva, San Antonio, San Bernardo, Los Reyes, El Venado, Las Lagunas, El Alamo, Palo Blanco, El Nogal, Chilicote, Rancho de Lemus, El Alamillo, Noria de Encinillas, Santa Rosa, Ojo del Buey, Potrero del Coronel, Victorino, Maxalca, Nieto, Guarachi, Cueva, Torreón, Durazno, La Estacada, San Pedro, Chuvizca, Chibato, Vallecillo, Los Charcos, El Embudo, El Torreoncillo, La Calera, Mapula, Potrero de la Griega, Mesa de Carretas, Corral de Piedra, Soto, La Silla, Sierrita de San Pedro, Cienega de los Padres, El Ojito, Potrero de la Domínguez, Rancho de Sierra, Potrero de la Herran, Sierra del Burreon, Chorreras, Las Pintas, Hormigas, Escondida, Pastor de la Escondida, Coyame, Sierra de los Arados, Potrero de Ubineta, Agua Sarca, Cañada de Juan Largo, Muralla, Cañada de la Mula, Alamillo de las Cruces, Cañon de los Cerros Colorados, Aranzazú, Namiquipa, Cañada del Oso, Sierra de San Phelipe, Picacho de Sierra, Vilchis, Tazcate, Metate, Tepehuanes, Quemada, Rincón, Elvira, San Diego, Cañada de Miguel, Valle de Santa Clara, Sierra de Enmedio, Carcay, La Escondida, Cañada de Guadalupe, and the others that are found in a westerly direction.

186. In an easterly direction they should reconnoiter, and with sufficient troops, Cuatro Cienegas; and arriving at the area of the Bolsón de Mapimí, which is next to the province of Coahuila, they will carry out the following operations.

187. Camp will be set up in El Potrero, from which place one squad will set out to the south to reconnoiter as much as possible the vicinity of Parras and the intervening watering places, doing the same to the west to a distance of 20 or 25 leagues. Having finished this they will examine the springs that are nearby like those of El Potrero, Calaveras, Agua Verde, and others, breaking camp to camp at the Ojo del Capulin, from where they will survey the Entrada de Sardinas and Boca de Aura. Having finished this, a squad will go out to reconnoiter to the west to a distance of 25 to 30 leagues, and having returned, it will continue its march in order to make camp at the Ojo del Carrisalexo, entering via the aforementioned westerly direction from which place [another squad] will go out to reconnoiter the interval that exists as far as the Tinaja del

Temaute. Having done this, they will continue their march via El Cañon de Zacate de Enjalma, and the two squads will continue with one entering by the pass and the other along the canyon, both of those squads attempting to join together at the Hacienda de San Joseph, at the Charcos de San Pedro, or in the Ojo de Santa María, with the understanding that it seems better to me at San Joseph if there be sufficient water, because from this place it is closer for the examination of the Puerto del Espadín, Aguage de San Eugenio, and to come out via the Puerto de Santa Theresa to the aforementioned Agua de Santa María, and for reconnoitering the land that lies between this Puerto and the Sierra de la Cuesta de los Capitanes, examining the Aguages de San Bartholomé, La Salada, and others until arriving at El Paso de San Vizente on the Río Grande del Norte, from where it will return via the same places to the province of Coahuila.

188. Since offensive war has peace as its objective, and since the wellbeing and conversion of the gentile Indians and the tranquillity of the frontier lands is of greatest attention, it will always be borne in mind that the most effective means of achieving such useful and pious ends are vigor and activity in war and good faith and gentleness in the treatment of the conquered, taken either in peace or as prisoners.

189. In my opinion both objectives can be achieved provided it is deemed expedient to invade simultaneously all the land that the treacherous Apaches occupy from east to west and from south to north by means of 10 detachments which will be deployed in the following way.

Detachments or Divisions That Can Be Formed for the General Campaign

190. The detachment of Coahuila, which must be the first, can be composed of 25 men from each of the presidios of San Juan Bautista del Río

Grande del Norte, Monclova, Santa Rosa, and San Antonio Bucareli; 100 friendly Indians and 50 citizens; and in all composing (including the subordinate officers which from these presidios they consider proper to select for command of their respective squads) the number of 275 men.

191. The second detachment will be composed of 30 men of the Presidio de San Sabá, including an officer; 25 from that of San Carlos; 25 from that of the Junta de los Ríos, and another equal number from that of El Príncipe; which in all comprise 105 men.

192. The third detachment will be composed of 40 men of the Presidio de San Elezeario and 100 citizens and Indian auxiliaries who for this purpose can be sent to it from the pueblo of El Paso del Norte; and in all consist of 140 men.

193. The fourth detachment can be formed of 200 men and 100 friendly Indians of the militia of the pueblo of El Paso del Río del Norte who willingly make these campaigns for the payment in booty; and in total consist in number of 300 effective men.

194. The fifth and sixth detachments can consist in New Mexico of the citizens and friendly Indians that are found in that province and who because of their location are not lacking for frontier defense against the Comanche Indians.

195. The seventh detachment can be formed of the 46 men of which the mobile company of Sonora is composed, provided that it is not earlier eliminated; 25 from each of the six presidios of its command and 150 Indians of the Opata nation; who all combined compose the number of 346 effective individuals.

196. The eighth detachment, which the commander in chief should command in person in order to place him in the position of being able to communicate his orders promptly to the other detachments, can be composed of 60 dragoons; 250 men including the Indian auxiliaries of the mobile corps of the expedition; 25 individuals from each of the presidios of Carrizal, San Buenaventura, and Janos; and in total comprising the number of 385 effective men.

197. The ninth detachment can be formed of one of the companies of the mobile corps of the expedition, whose number of men is 125 including its 25 Indian auxiliaries.

198. The tenth and last detachment can be formed of 50 men including some Indian auxiliaries.

Routes That Should Be Followed by the Detachments Named for the Offensive War or General Campaign

199. The first detachment will carry out its departure from the Presidio de Agua Verde on the assigned day, directing its march via Las Bacas on the banks of the Río Grande del Norte to where the Río San Pedro joins it, and from the headwaters of the latter it will continue its route to the Río Colorado, inspecting along its march all the retreats, sierras, canyons, and watering places that are found both to its right and its left with all the minuteness, prudence, and caution that is required to surprise (if it is possible) the Indians where they may be gathered together.

200. The second detachment will prepare its departure from the Presidio de las Juntas de los Ríos Norte y Conchos, directing its march to El Alamo, La Cienega de San Jacinto, the Puerto de la Peña Blanca, Tazcate, Agua Delgada, Las Adargas, which place is located at a distance of one-eighth of a league from the Río Colorado, along whose banks it will travel to La Rinconada, or the place where this river joins with the Río Grande del Norte, it being probable that in this passage it will find the Coahuila camp, noting that in all the previous ones water and pasture are found, in addition to the great advantage of being equivalent day's journeys and all over flat land.

201. The third detachment will set out from the Presidio de San Elezeario, headed to the Sierra de Guadalupe, via the Caxón Grande, La Tinaja, Carrizo, La Salineta la Grande, Guadalupe, and inspecting along its route La Cola del Aguila, Sierra del Diablo, that of El Mogano and its range, and it will wait in the Sierra de Guadalupe or in its vicinity for new orders concerning what it should carry out.

202. The fourth detachment will leave via Los Organos, Petaca, reconnoitering all that cordillera as far as Sierra Blanca, where it will join with the New Mexico camp, indispensably having to be in that sierra on the day that it was deemed convenient to set.

203. The fifth detachment, which must leave from New Mexico, will direct its march via the Sierra Obscura to the Blanca, where it will join with the fourth detachment, with both remaining in that place until new orders and for the purpose of preventing the retreat of Indians who might flee from the battlefield and go to the Mimbres and the Sierra de Gila, the detachment adjusting its marches in such a way as to effect its arrival at the aforementioned Sierra Blanca the day that was set as being opportune.

204. The sixth detachment, which must also leave from New Mexico, will direct its march along the back side of the Sierra de los Ladrones, inspecting the Sierra de la Magdalena and heading to that of Fray Cristóbal on the western side. It will remain in that spot until further orders, having also carried out its arrival there the same day that it had been opportune to arrange beforehand with the previous detachments four and five, in order to prevent the retreat via the aforementioned place of the Indians who might flee from the other battlefields.

205. The seventh detachment will direct its march via the Sierra de Chiricagui, hugging the Río Gila and going into the sierra of the same name, it will continue until hitting the Río Grande del Norte where it will remain until the arrival of the commander in chief, trying to carry out its [arrival] at the said place on the day it was opportune to establish if the events that might arise during the march should permit it.

206. The eighth detachment from the Presidio de San Buenaventura will direct its march via the Corral de Piedra, La Florida, El Cerro Gordo,

hugging La Sangre de Christo, Corral de San Agustín, to go down to the Muerto on the Río Grande del Norte, where it will meet with the seventh detachment on the same day as was set, and afterward it will continue its march to the Sierra Blanca, that of Sacramento, and of Guadalupe, not only with a view toward getting information concerning the progress achieved by the camps stationed at said places, but also to dictate measures for them for continuation of the war.

207. With due care that behind the presidios there are no longer any enemies who during campaign operations might attack the interior of the provinces, the ninth detachment will leave via the Bolsón de Mapimí and reconnoitering in great detail its sierras and watering places, and especially those of Acatita la Grande, and that of Baxan, it will continue its march to the Sierra de la Paila, and the vicinity of Parras. Upon its return via the province of Coahuila to the city of Chihuahua, it will reconnoiter El Carrizalexo, La Tinaja del Temaute, via the Cañon de Zacate de Enxalma, Ojo de Santa María, Puerto del Espadín, Aguage de San Eugenio, and leaving via El Puerto de Santa Theresa to the Aguage de Santa María, reconnoitering the intermediate land from this Puerto to La Cuesta de los Capitanes, inspecting the Aguage de la Salada, etc. as far as El Paso de San Vicente, and from here it will head via the Presidio de San Carlos, La Mula, Potrero de la Herran, to the city of Chihuahua, to whose commander an account of the progress achieved during the expedition under his command should be given.

208. The tenth and last detachment will leave from the city of Chihuahua headed to the Sierra de Santa Clara, the valley of this same name, and from here it will continue its march reconnoitering all the sierras that there are as far as the Río de Temehuaque; and after having reported to the captain of the Presidio de Janos concerning the events that had occurred on its expedition, it will return to its own city, awaiting new orders concerning what it must do.

209. Each and every one of the aforementioned detachments should be found in the lands that are assigned to each on the days that are predetermined and for no reason will they vary from the specified routes, except only in the case of finding some trace of the enemy which they must follow if fresh or not very old, and if they should succeed in overtaking them and after investigating find that the [Indian] forces are not

superior, they should attack without any delay, except if they can arrange to surprise them the following day.

210. If the number of barbarians be excessive and the terrain that they occupy is extremely advantageous, and because they are gathered together there may be time to be joined with the nearby detachment or detachments, opportune word will be given provided, in accordance with the itinerary assigned to each detachment, the distances and places where they might be found can be taken into consideration.

211. The commanders of the detachments must keep an accurate diary of the most important events on their expeditions and of the engagements they will succeed in having with the enemies, and in this case they will go into detail about the place and other circumstances, taking very special pains in the case of the prisoners that they might take, even to the point if opportunity allows of being able to send them to the nearest presidio; the documents of which they will send to the commander in chief so that through them he becomes informed of the operations of each one and that his measures stem from them.

212. In consideration of the fact that by the itinerary the commanders can estimate the time they will be on campaign, they will be able to allot the corresponding supplies, distributing them in such a way that there will never occur a case of a soldier lacking his daily ration which in accordance with the ordinances must be issued to him, and for its fulfillment they will give the corresponding orders at the proper time to the respective supply officers.

213. The aforementioned commanders will not omit any measure conducive to achievement of the worthwhile ends to which such useful effort is aimed, as in this way the lands of the enemy will be explored in greater detail; they will be able to pursue them often without delay; encounters and confrontations with the squads or groups of them will be necessary; they will observe the watchfulness and steadiness with which our troop maintains itself in the field; they will not enter our lands freely; they will find in the rigor of our arms the just punishment they deserve; with a result from all this being the tranquillity of the frontiers.

214. For command of those detachments, there should be selected from among the frontier captains those most active and knowledgeable of the

lands involved; of the ideas and cunning of the enemies; and of the places where they usually lie in ambush; persons of known valor and knowledge of the way of making war against the Indians, determining the day in which all the detachments must carry out their campaign departure, which will doubtless be all the same from the presidios and places that are indicated.

Special Campaigns

215. In addition to the general campaign, they will carry out other special ones against the Western Apaches who inhabit the sierras of Chiricagui, Gila, and that of the Mimbres, from which the immoderate colds of the months of December, January, and February oblige them therefore to seek refuge in other areas of more moderate temperature.

216. The punishment of those [Indians] can be completely carried out, arranging departure in the months of February or March from the Presidio de Janos of three competent squads in the following way.

217. The first squad should direct its march downstream to Las Viznagas, the place called La Espía, La Boca de Guzmán, Carrizal, Saucitos, and El Alemán, where it will await the arrival of the second and third.

218. The second squad should leave on the same day that the first has done, following its march via La Palotada, to the Sierra de Enmedio, San Luis, via El Peñol de Don Gabriel, to arrive at El Alemán, where it will join with the preceding one.

219. The third should make its departure three days later than have the first and second, following its march via the Punta del Mal País to La Palotada, Ojo del Perro, Ojo de Beitia, to hit the slope of the Sierra de la Hacha at El Alemán where it will join with the others.

220. Once united the three squads will reconnoiter in detail the Sierra de la Hacha and in the greatest silence possible so as not to be heard beforehand by the enemies, where, as in the other indicated places, they will surely find the enemies occupied making mescal, which forms a

great part of their subsistence. Once provided with what they need of it for their use, they retire with their families to the Sierra de los Mimbres in the middle of the month of April to plant their corn, beans, and squash in the canyons of that same sierra, which time seems equally opportune for punishment, and could be achieved by means of a detachment composed of at least 250 men commanded by an officer familiar with those lands.

221. To shoot with skill, to load quickly, to maintain formation, to break it and to reunite in order to sustain each other, maintaining proper silence, should be considered the maneuvers sufficient for the type of enemies against whom this troop sees action, and its individuals are well instructed in them.

222. Provided it is deemed desirable to increase some of the frontier troops, from practical knowledge from the Indian wars that helps me, I deem as most proper for the purpose those who are recruited and enlisted in those lands, because they are those who with less difficulty adjust themselves to the extraordinary hardship of this warfare, totally different from that of the rest of civilized people in consideration of not being able to observe any other instruction than their own to combat the Indians.

223. It consists of being skillful men on horseback; knowing how to fire a shotgun; using the shield, which is something natural with them; traveling with fortitude many leagues by day and by night; suffering, sun, lack of sleep, rain and snow without any more food at times than a little ground corn dissolved in water that they call pinole, nor any greater covering shelter than that offered by a cloak. In this way it will be possible to make up for the lack of Catalonian riflemen whom I requested from the government [in a letter] dated 8 March 1774.

224. In the war waged against the Apaches, I will always deem it useful to use the extremely loyal Opata Indians, both for their proven bravery as well as for their great knowledge of the land, sierras, and watering places where the Western Apache Indians live. For sorties to be made they will make themselves ready in the numbers and at the times that the commander will determine, as there has never been an instance in which they failed to fulfill any order of those given to them, showing on

all occasions the constant love that they profess toward the Spaniards. These acts, together with their dedication to farming, the eagerness with which they attempt to teach Christian doctrine to their children, and their special decorum in divine worship, makes them in my opinion deserving to be looked after and viewed with love, distinguishing them for the other nations.

225. Having thus detailed all of the provisions that I consider conducive to defensive and offensive war against the Apaches, there remains only the presentation of the idea that I have of the Indians who are congregated in pueblos and missions according to their provinces, without forgetting the damage that some of them cause in the interior [of the provinces].

226. In that of Sonora, besides the Opata nation, there are the Seri, Pimas Altos and Bajos, the Tiburones, and the Yaqui Indians. As a result of the military expedition of Sonora, the Seris and Pimas Altos have congregated in the pueblos of El Pitic, Pitiqui, Caborca, Visanic, San Antonio de Oquitoa, El Ati, Santa Theresa, Tubutama, Saric, San Xavier del Wac [Bac], and San Agustín del Tuquison, and I saw them all when I was in the province with evidence, according to my opinion, of remaining peaceful and faithful and most of them dedicated to agriculture, except for some 20 families that deserted the land and to whom has been attributed some damage that has happened; and none is reported done by the Tiburones for a long time according to the reports of the provincial heads that exist in the Archive of Chihuahua.

227. Much quieter and more agreeable, the Yaqui nation is employed continually in the Real de la Cieneguilla and other mining areas of Sonora, to which they are much inclined. The Pimas Bajos live peacefully in their towns near the Presidio de San Miguel Horcasitas with great application in the working of their farm lands and in commerce that they have with the Spaniards.

228. In the province of Nueva Vizcaya live in various towns the vast, large nations of the Tarahumara Alta and Baja, and these disguised as Apaches are those who commit much damage in its interior; but these excesses, if I am not mistaken, stem from the lack of order in the settlements, and in the oppression with which they are treated. Although

it is stipulated by law that the orders given are for a third of the Indians in each case, grave excesses are committed so that there are times when nobody remains in the town to take care of the families of the absent ones.

229. Along with the tyrannical prejudice is the poor pay by the landowners and the worse manner in which they are treated and how, due to their absence at the necessary times of planting and harvesting, they reach the point of lack of sustenance. Seeing their families naked and starving, it is not strange that set on seeking aid, they commit thefts and do other harm in order to meet their need, falling into the error of committing many murders so as not to be found out.

230. The superior government has issued repeated measures for the setting in order of these towns with the proper view of guarding against such excesses; but this will never be achieved as long as the *justicia* of each one does not investigate everyday the whereabouts of the Indians; and measures are taken to contain them peacefully under the orders given according to the laws. I consider this matter to be of the utmost attention and preference because, if not resolved, damages will always take place in the province, and without knowing for sure who commits them although in general they are attributed to the Apache.

231. In the province of Coahuila there are various Indian towns, but only the Julimeños have up to now given reason for misgivings by their constant friendship with the Apaches. It is necessary to watch greatly their conduct to know if they are the authors of many robberies and other excesses that have been attributed to them; but in order to live without such care, I will always believe it to be proper that they be made to return to their old pueblo of Julimes in Nueva Vizcaya, under a faithful person who can watch over their movements and report promptly.

232. In the province of New Mexico, which is located more than a degree beyond our line, there are the Jemes, Silla [Zia], Santa Ana, Sandia, Isleta, Pueblo de Genízaros,[30] Laguna, Acoma, the Navajos, and other Indians that I do not know, but I do know that all dedicate themselves peacefully to the agriculture of their lands and the raising of major and minor livestock, from which they profit in such a great abundance that rare is the year in which there are fewer than 2,000 head that they send

30. Although there were several *genízaro* towns in New Mexico, the context here makes it almost certain that Tomé is the one indicated in the list.

for sale to the presidios of the line, as well as other goods such as stockings, blankets, and cloth, demonstrating thereby their hard work.

233. Near the pueblo of El Paso del Norte there are four other towns of Indians known by the names of Piros, Mansos, Zumas, and Tiguas who live under the greatest control of the missionary ministers and of the *justicia ordinaria*, working their farm lands and especially in the cultivation of vines which are abundant in those lands; and although all are suited for warfare because of their demonstrated valor and knowledge of the sierras and watering places where the Apaches live in those directions, the sorties that they voluntarily make against them never produce favorable results as a consequence of the lack of the Detachment of El Robledo called for in the new Royal Instruction, the establishment of which has been suspended up until now by the reports made by Brigadier Don Pedro Fermín de Mendinueta.[31]

31. Pedro Fermín de Mendinueta, a native of the Spanish province of Navarre, became governor of New Mexico in early 1767 and served for over a decade. He was particularly active in Indian campaigns. He was replaced by Juan Bautista de Anza and departed in March of 1778. His suggestion had been not to have a garrison at El Robledo, but rather to establish it farther north at Socorro.

234. That of Texas, which is also found more than a degree beyond our line, has been of the overseas possessions of Spain the most costly, although of very little utility; the largest, although unknown, and the one that has produced the most hostilities; but the one of greatest importance on many counts, since none of the others can match it. It borders on the east that of Louisiana, or New Orleans; on the west, the Río Medina; on the north the Missouri; and on the south the sea or Gulf of Mexico. It has abundant rivers that water it; sierras that surround it and protect it; valleys and plains that rightly call for farmers; and it is peopled by numerous gentiles who when attracted to recognition and vassalage of the monarchy would make it more fertile and richer than the other provinces because of its location, multitude of people, and fine climate.

235. The Indians who live there under the protection of our presidios and pass for friends are the Texas, Orcoquisac, Vidaes, Asinaix, Navedachos, Yatasis, and Caudachos, all of the same language. There are also the Tehuacanes, Yxcanis and Taovayas, who although they seem to be three tribes, make up one people, even though separated into an equal number of factions. And these are those who are principally blamed for the outbreaks committed in past years against the Presidio de San Sabá, and there is no lack of those who confirm that they have been provoked into it by oppression and other mistreatment.

236. Although they may not be our true friends, they are without doubt friends of the other nations; they love each other, and in addition to the union that is a result of their bartering, there is among them another political reason that will never allow the separation of their interests, and it would be advantageous to attract the aforementioned three *rancherías* by good means so that they be friendly, and thereby block the way of the restless Guazas and other bellicose Indians of the north that border on the English possessions, which greedy nation would like nothing better than to penetrate into those parts.

237. To the west of the Tuacanes, Yxcanis, and Taovayas are the Comanches, natives and lords of the wide land that is enclosed by the cordilleras of New Mexico and the abundant Missouri River; a multitude so large and haughty that they consider themselves equal in number to the stars. They are skillful in handling the horse and the lance, and of great dexterity in shooting arrows; they always live in tents, wandering from one place to another without staying longer than they need to, and from hunting alone they provide themselves with deer and buffalo from which they get their food and clothing.

238. The necessity in which they found themselves previously of asking each for permission to go through the lands of the Tuacanes, Yxcanis, and Taovayas was the reason that the Comanches did not make more than a momentary and restless stop there, because they viewed those nations as the domain of a powerful enemy from whom they always received fatal blows due to the range of the rifle. But later with all of them [the Comanches] confederated, free of their apprehensions and with equal arms, they are now spreading as a mob from the remotest part of the north to the most southerly country, seemingly taking revenge in that way on that obstacle they had experienced for such a long time.

239. Also the Apaches, who blocked the path of the Comanches because of being in the way, are (although opponents of each other) every one of them enemies of our provinces of Texas and New Mexico where they have committed bloody attacks; and among all the nations mentioned, it is the most feared, both because of the firearms acquired from the English which they know how to use skillfully, as well as for their valor and intrepidity, and because they usually never flee, preferring rather

to die or overcome; from which and from the method they have of waging war, they have given in these recent times much proof of being more civilized and political than the rest of their barbarian neighbors.

240. To the south or better said on the Gulf of Mexico coast, next to the Presidio de la Bahía del Espíritu Santo, lives grouped together the Karankawa nation, who, if up until now they have caused little trouble, have lately shown the detriment that their being nearby is for those who are cast ashore on [this coast], against whom they have committed many inhumanities. At present Captain Luis Cazorla[32] seems to have them as friends, or in a kind of subordination; however, they continue unconverted and serve as a shelter for the apostates of those missions. It seems to me appropriate that they be persuaded to be missionized or that they be forced, since they are few, to live with the other neophytes; because not being able to be useful in the wrecks of vessels that frequently run ashore on that coast, it is better that those who save themselves find it uninhabited than be left to fall into their hands to become a sacrifice—thereby avoiding the erection of a fort recently considered, to which I was opposed in my opinion, as can be seen by the documents in the Archive of Chihuahua.

241. If its establishment should have for its objective that proposed by Don Luis Cazorla, it would certainly be useful to the mariners amidst the dangers that abound on that coast, but perhaps with it the way would be open for illegal trade which the province of Texas does not much need in view of their having it on many sides due to the nearness of the English and French, which reason is the same that I had and will always have to argue against the settlement of Nuestra Señora del Pilar de Bucareli in the place where it is, because being located in the midst of the infidel nations mentioned, it receives by means of all of them whatever goods the province consumes and others that are introduced in those nearby which are their neighbors, without the measures for correction of such damage up to now having been sufficient.

242. I have lingered in my description of this province and its inhabitants much more than in that of the others because it is less known and because of it being the sole bastion that this New Spain has against the two powers of England and France. I have deemed it proper to point it out that, if with my notes and the other information that you acquire

32. Luis Cazorla was captain of the presidio of Bahía del Espíritu Santo and of San Antonio Bucareli in 1772. In 1778 while serving as inspector of troops in Coahuila, he was named interim governor of Texas. In 1783 Cazorla was again captain of Bahía del Espíritu Santo.

Your Lordship should determine to apply your endeavors to making it happy, subduing as many Indians as can be attracted to vassalage, then they will have little to fear from the inhabitants since the wide extent of land that they inhabit would be the greatest problem.

243. I think that with what has been explained I have fulfilled considerably the desire of Your Lordship both so you may know the state in which I found the frontiers when I received command of them, as well as what was done in all of its lands and the setup I left in them.

244. It has only been possible to achieve the difference noted from one time to the other at the cost of considerable expenditure from the public treasury; of my zeal; and of the toil of the troop. Today it has an invincible superiority over the barbarians. Previously a few of them would have dared [attack] if we were triple their number; and now everything happens to the contrary as a result of the repeated attacks that they have received.

245. Nevertheless, attacks, robberies, deaths, and other hostilities will never be lacking on the frontiers, since it is not easy to prevent totally the Indians' entry that some troublesome ones are accustomed astutely to carry out without being noticed by the squads. But if the patrols are well organized and the most suspicious places are occupied by detachments, [the frontiers] will be greatly improved, will have them restrained, and will have those settlements and towns at peace, which is of interest to the treasury and to the public.

246. The plan that I propose in this report is what my experiences taught me, what I ordered to be done, and what was successful in my limited efforts. No matter how bad they might be, they will no doubt give Your Lordship insight of great utility and importance to the service. But having no interest that they continue and even less that other measures which I bring to light should serve as a guide, it is up to Your Lordship to take for your proper action what you judge advantageous and attainable.

May Our Lord guard Your Lordship many years. Mexico, 22 July 1777. Your most attentive and certain servant kisses the hand of Your Lordship. [Signed] Don Hugo Oconor. [To] Señor Don Theodoro de Croix.

Tables

Account That Indicates the Effective Force of the Four Militia Companies Recruited in the Pueblo of El Paso del Norte

Companies	Capts.	Lts.	Ens.	Sgts.	Cpls.	Pvts.	Total
First	1	1	1	1	4	45	53
Second	1	1	1	1	4	45	53
Third	1	1	1	1	4	45	53
Fourth	1	1	1	1	4	45	53
	4	4	4	4	16	180	212

Mexico, 22 July 1777

Facsimile of the
Original Document

Nº

Hugo Oconôr.—

Informe sobre los *[ilegible]*
del *[ilegible]* de Nueva España *[ilegible]*
el Virrey Marques de Croix 1771
[ilegible]

Estado que manifiesta con distincion de Provincias, el numero de Presidios de que se compone la nueva Linea formada de Mar, á Mar, barre la defensa de sus Fronteras; la fuerza efectiva de sus Guarniciones con distincion de Clases. El Methodo de Cavalleria y Municion, y el annual que para cada Presidio, segun lo dispuesto por los Real Instruccion de 10. de Septiembre de el Año pasado de 1772.

Presidios	Capitanes	Thenientes	Alferezes	Capellanes	1er Sarg.	Caros	Soldados	Indios pueblos	Fuerza total	Situación de municion	Ydem utilizada	Situacion de cada Presidio
					1	2	65		52	357	51	19.130.0.0
					2	6	63		81	567	51	29.580.0.0
					1	2	40	10	57	352	51	18.998.6
					1	2	40	10	56	352	51	18.998.6
					1	2	40	10	57	352	51	18.998.6
					1	2	40	10	57	352	51	18.998.6
					1	2	40	10	57	352	51	18.998.6
					1	2	40	10	57	352	51	18.998.6
					1	2	40	10	57	352	51	18.998.6
					1	2	40	10	57	352	51	18.998.6
					1	2	40	10	57	352	51	18.998.6
					1	2	40	10	57	352	51	18.998.6
					1	2	40	10	57	352	51	18.998.6
					1	2	40	10	57	352	51	18.998.6
					1	2	40	10	55	352	51	18.998.6
					1	2	40	10	57	352	51	18.998.6
					1	2	40	10	56	352	51	18.998.6
					1	2	40	10	55	352	51	18.998.6
					1	2	40		45	322	46	47.630.0.0
					1	2	40		45	322	46	17.630.0.0
					1	2	40		45	322	46	45.230.0.0
					2	6	98		110	560	80	35.680.0.0
22	19	23	19	15	24	52	972	160	1284	8082	1166	438.960 p.

Plaza maior

Plaza maior		Pesos
Comte. Inspr. el Cax.l B.r Dn. Pedro Pablo		3000
tes.r nes. El Capn. ô Brigadr de More.		3000
el ofisal Insp.r El cap.n Dn.		3000
		14.000 p.

Nota.

Otra.

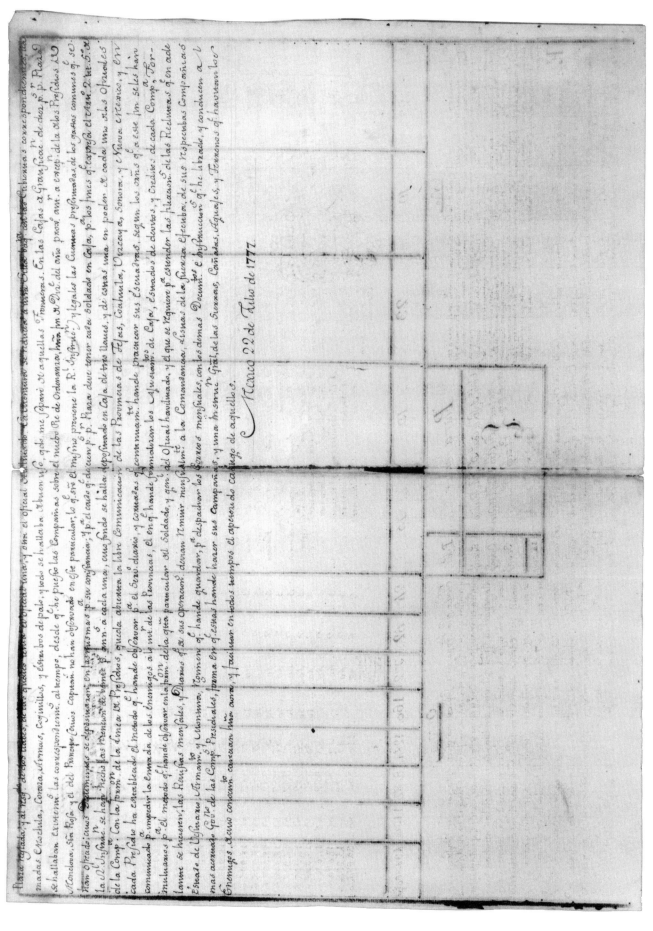

(Reduced)

Estado que manifiesta la Fuerza efectiva de que se componen las quatro Compañias del Cuerpo Volante de la Expedicion y las dos Piquetes de Dragones, que sirven el servicio en las Fronteras de Provincias internas, con expresion de los nombres de sus Oficiales, distincion de Sargentos, Tambores, Cavos, Soldados, è Yndios Auxiliares; total de cada una, situado de Camisada, y Avituallada, y el haver an.l que gozan.

Comp.s y Piquetes	Capitanes	Prim.s Tenientes	Segundos ten.tes	Prim.s Alferezes	Sarg.tos	Tambor.s	Cavos	Soldad.s	Yndios Auxil.	Ydals d Paisanos	Situado d Cav.	Idem d Soldad.	Haver an.l q gozan
Primera	D. Domº Diaz	D. Josef de la O	D. Antonio Villa	D. Ramon Mexaxejo	2	—	4	83	25	125	675	112	32.623.7
Segunda	D. Juan de la Rambla	D. Josef Carvajales	Vacante	D. Ubo. Ortega	2	—	4	83	45	144	735	122	34.746.0
Tercera	D. Joh Montoya	D. Tomas Oxeda	Vacante	D. Dom. Mariano	2	—	4	83	25	124	675	112	32.623.7
Quarta	D. Juan Almaral	D. Tomas Guzcolo	D. Felix Pachea	D. Juan Jph Padilla	2	—	4	83	25	125	675	112	32.623.7
Piq.te de Pino.l Esp.a	D. Jph Gaxiola Yga	D. Jose Chacon		D. Mig.l Subidan	2	1	4	43	—	53	318	53	14.982.0
Id. de Mexico	D. Jose chacon			D. Matheo Garcia	2	1	4	43	—	32	318	53	14.962.0
Mexico	**6**	**5**	**2**	**6**	**12**	**2**	**24**	**442**	**120**	**623**	**3396**	**561**	**162.581,5**

Plana Mayor:

	Pesos
Ayud.te m.or D.n Juan Miguel de Urrea	660
Id. D.n	660
	1.320

Fue toda esta Tropa, est.n sup. calidad, así en Talle, como en Robustez, Valor y constancia comp. separan las incomparables Jompas de su demás, muy ufanos en manejos à cav.º y en aquellas evolucion viriles, y adaptables a la especie de Guerra q.e hazen, y muy inferiores en los Terrenos que recorren los Enemigos.

En el total haver de esta Tropa estan comprehendidos los haveres r.s mensuales concedidos a cada Plaza de Guerra, desde el Sargento inclusive, para la Gratificacion de Cavallos, y las raciones de Campaña q.e se suministran en especie a los Individuos de los dos Piquetes de Dragones.

El Vestuario de que usa la Tropa es uniforme en todas, y consta de una Chupa azul con una pequeño buelta y collarin encarnado, bohon dorado, Calzon de Tripe azul, Capa de paño del mismo color, Carruchera, Cuera, y Vandolera de Gamuza, en la que se halla bordado el numero de la Compañia, Corbatin negro, Sombrero, Zapatos, y botines, y todo se hallaba de buen uso, quando no me separe de aquellas Fronteras. El Armamento consfaba de espada ancha del Tamaño y hechura que usa la demás Cavalleria del Exercito, Lanzas, Adarga, Escopeton y Pistolas, del que de orden del Rey, se ha remudo, à aquellas Fronteras para el uso de sus Presidios, y descontando su total importe, à favor de la R.l Hacienda por el Thesorero de la Villa de Chihuahua D.n Manuel Antonio de Escorza.

Mexico 22. de Julio de 1777.

(Reduced)

[v]

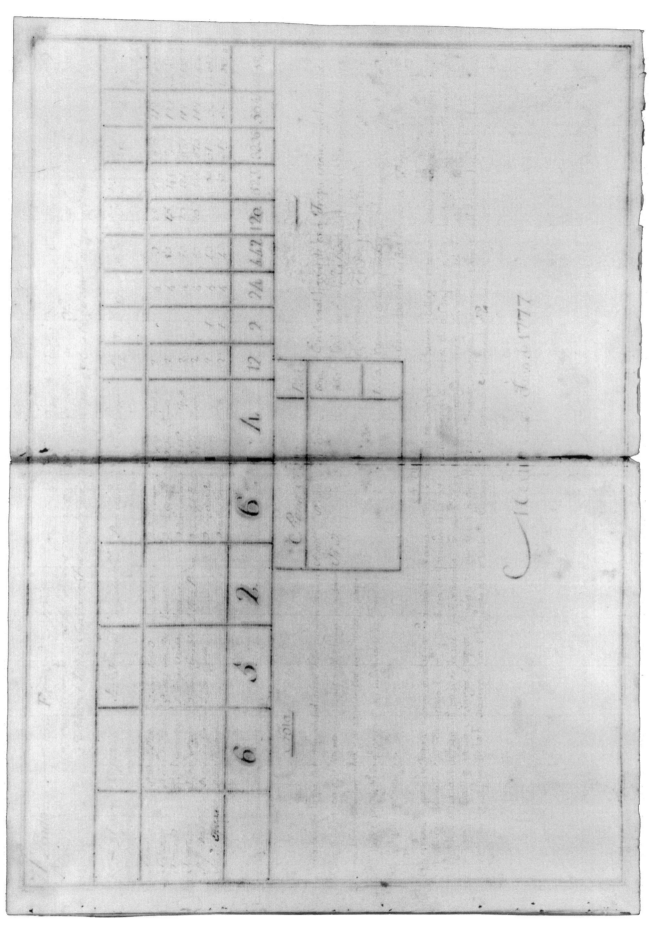

(Reduced)

Estado que manifiesta la Fuerza efectiva de las quatro Compañías de Milicias formadas en el Pueblo de el Páso de el Norte.

Compañías.	Capitan.s	Tenient.s	Alferez.os	Sarg.tos	Cavos	Soldad.s	Total.
Primera	1	1	1	1	4	45	53
Segunda	1	1	1	1	4	45	53
Tercera	1	1	1	1	4	45	53
Quarta	1	1	1	1	4	45	53
	4	4	4	4	16	180	212

Mexico 22. de Julio. de 1777.

Estado que manifiesta la Fábrica... ... ...
Compañías e Indios segun la... Plaza del Rio del...
Torre

Compañías							
Puebla	1	1	1	1	4	40	55
	1	1	1	1	4	40	55
	1	1	1	1	4	40	55
	1	1	1	1	4		55
	4	4	4	4	16		

México 22 de Abril
de 1777.

Mui Señor mio: en el Villete que pasò V.S. á mis manos con fecha de 17 de Mayo anterior, hallo incerta la Carta que parece aver V.S. dirigido à Chiguagua con fecha de 7. del proprio: y en ella dice V.S. que no obstante las copias que de mis oficios le hà pasado el Exmo Sr Virrey, desea que le instruia Yo particularmente de el estado en que hallè las fronteras delas Provincias de su mando: el en que quedaban quando dexè el mio: y de los medios que estimo utiles al progreso feliz de mis ideas, pues considerandolos (es honor que V.S. me hace) dirigidos con el acierto proprio de mi conocimiento, y experiencias, no duda V.S. le servirán de Norte para el govierno de sus providencias.

Bien sabia Yo que tal informe era consecuencia precisa de la entrega de el mando, especialmente à un Jefe como V.S. que no hà visto los terrenos que comprehende; bien que posea en completo quantas noticias hagan el de la mas fina theorica, pero como muchas disposiciones de V.S. llegaron à ellos con preferencia à su Villete, y aun mucho antes dela separacion mia; discurri con tal fundamento, ô que V.S. no necesitaba las luces que

[1]

pide le ministre, ò que seria ocioso mi trabajo por mas que à èl me animasse la creencia de su utilidad, el obsequio de V.S. y las ventajas de el servicio.

Estas reflexiones que fueron causa parcial de mi inaccion hasta à hora hè unido despues à la de el desayre que sufririan los informes de mis experiencias sabiendo las disposiciones dictadas en las Frontera, acaso por aver preferido otras mas solidas en el concepto, y estimacion de V.S. y à la verdad no entiendo como esto se combine con el honor que en su papel indica dispensarme de querer tomar mis reglas para norte de sus providencias, quando yà son tantas las dictadas sin oirme.

Confirmado assi, lo que puedo esperar de la acceptacion de V.S, deberia Yo retraerme de dar dictamen en asunto que tan poco aprecio se hace de mi voto, y mucho menos de referir lo que concibo practicable para la continuacion progresiva de mis felices ideas, siendo assi que las de V.S. son opuestas, y diferentes en todo, como me consta, acaso por que en su practica confia mejores successos; y Yo celebraré estos ciertamente por que deséo los adelantamientos del servicio, y las satisfacciones de V.S.

Sin embargo impeliendome mi propria buena inclinacion à cooperar à ellas por lo que à V.S. estimo, y por que à mas de el servicio del

Rey merecen toda la mia unas Provincias, cuios terrenos hé pisado sin perdonar fatiga, y cuia seguridad hé pretendido à costa de muchos riesgos, y necesidades por quantos medios me pudo animar el zelo de el servicio, è inspirar el amor que las profeso; haré à V.S. una relacion circunstanciada de lo acaecido en el tiempo de mi mando, por si los sucessos, disposiciones, y demas de que haré mension, conduxessen à V.S. para noticia, quando no para sus aciertos.

Hallabasse por fines de el año de 1771 el Capitan d.n Bernardo de Galvez con el comando de las Armas de Nueva Vizcaya; y resuelto el Govierno à relevarle de èl, para que pudiera regresar à España con su tio el Ill.mo S.or d.n Joseph de Galvez, seme confio à mi este encargo por Decreto de 10. de Septiembre con dos mil pesos de sobre sueldo, ô gratificacion en calidad de ayuda de costa.

Quando Yo recibi la citada orden, sabia yà venir marchando à esta Capital el actual Señor Virrey Fr. d.n Antonio Bucareli, y Ursua, destinado à succeder al Exmo S.or Marques de Croix: y pareciendome justo esperar su arribo, por si sobre las con que me hallaba, tenia algunas otras advertencias que hacerme, lo executé assi persuadido de que todo convenia para afianzar el acierto de tan grave comision.

Con tal deseo me presenté al nuevo Virrey à los tres dias de su llegada: puse en sus manos la citada orden,

y hecho cargo de el obgeto de ella, no solo aprobó
las disposiciones de su antecesor, sino que con fecha
de 4. de Octubre de el mismo año, me previno en
una suia lo que importaba mi traslacion à Chiqu-
agua, encargandome estrechamente el desempeño de
aquella Comandancia, con la calidad de dar parte
por los Correos de quanto ocurriesse.

9.   Dispuesta mi marcha, me transferi à la Villa
de Chiguaqua, como en donde debia tomar el mando dela frontera: y aunque arribé à ella el 17.de
Diciembre de dho año, no pude verificarlo harta
el 19. por hallarse el Capitan dn Bernardo Galvez en campaña.

10.   Dediqueme desde luego à tomar instruccion
de el estado de las Provincias demi mando, y en
especial dela nueva Vizcaya, y hallé esta mas
que todas consternada por las continuas incursiones de los Apaches, cuio terror llegaba al
ultimo estremo: y quando de todo me parecio
tener completas noticias, hize presente al
Govierno la calidad delos males que padecio
aquella Provincia, y el fatal deplorable estado
à que la encontré reducida, desde el año de 1748.
en que se continuaba la Guerra con porfia,
llevando siempre los Apaches casi todo el
triunfo de lo que intentaban: perdiendo el
Rey mucha copia de caudales; dexando ilu-
sorias las providencias, y conatos de el Govierno, y con poco honor las armas de S. M.

11.   La narracion de los destrozos, robos, muertes, y otras clases de daños que entonces hice presentes, parecerian à primera vista demasiado ponderados, ò efectos de el temor, ò fin particular de los informantes, pero à mas de identificarse en la realidad de ellos, constan todos por documentos harto fieles, que hè dexado en el Archivo de Chiguagua.

12.   Son irrefragable, y visible prueba de esta verdad los Pueblos de Indios, y Españoles: Guarachi, S.n Juan, S.n Antonio, S.ta Rita, S.ta Rosa, Namiquipa, las Cruces, y S.n Luis, situados al Norte, y Poniente de la Villa de Chiguagua: el Valle de S.ta Clara, las opulentas Haciendas Casas Grandes, Torreon de Amoloya, las Cruces, S.n Miguel Namiquipa, Babicora, el Picacho, el Rincon de Terna, S.n Luis, Malanoche, la Laguna de Pacheco, Aguanueva, Hormigas, el Torreon de Guemes, el Sacramento, las Chorreras, y muchos Ranchos que avia en sus immediaciones: todo lo que se hallaba enteramente despoblado, por no aver podido resistir sus habitadores las continuadas invasiones de los Barbaros.

13.   El Valle de S.n Buenaventura, sostenido antes por Destacamentos de Soldados Presidiarios, y despues por el Presidio de su nombre, quedò totalmente destruido de los bienes de Campo, y desamparado de el Vecindario que le poblaba, por aver buscado su seguridad en la fuga. A la Hacienda del Carmen, cuias siembras, y crias

[5]

de Cavallada no pudieron libertarse de las manos de los Yndios, la hallè reducida à un corto laborio mui atrazado, por no tener mulada suficiente para la conduccion, y expendio de sus fructos. La del Carrizal que siempre se mantubo con el auxilio de un Destacamento para su defensa de orden del Govierno, sufrio no obstante, casi igual suerte. Y las Haciendas de Encinillas, en que se contaban antes mas de quarenta, y seis mil Reces, tendrian como unas ocho mil por el reiterado Robo, y destrozo de los Barbaros.

14.   Lloraban, esto, con razon, los moradores de aquellos Pueblos, y Valles, en que llevaban la maior parte los gruesos Hacenderos, y dueños de Ranchos, pues subiendo el numero de sus Ganados maiores à mas de trescientas mil Cabezas; el de Ganado menor à doscientas mil; y el de Cavallada, y mulada como à quatrocientas mil, por ser de cria las mas delas Haciendas, y tener mucho expendio, y consumo en las de beneficio de Platas, apenas poseian entonces una tercia parte.

15.   Por Oriente, y Sur de Chiguagua, se hallaban igualmente desamparadas varias Haciendas, y Poblaciones. Las del Sauz diez, y seis leguas de aquella Villa, en que estube alojado el dia antes de llegar à ella, acababa de padecer uno de los muchos insultos que los Yndios acostumbraban. No aviendo hallado en ella

Gente, rompieron las Puertas, la entraron à su arbitrio, destrozaron Escritorios, Mesas, Sillas, Caxon de Ornamentos, Capilla, y quantos muebles
hallaron en ella, por complemento de su ferocidad,
y desahogo de su venganza. La de S.n Antonio de
la Javonera, la de Ojes, la de Sapiain, la de el
Belduque, la Boca del Potrero de Dominguez, el
Pueblo de S.n Pedro, Julimes, y el Valle de Basuchil
padecian igualmente, y en este se hallaban des-
pobladas las Haciendas de S.n Ygnacio, de S.n Antonio de Padua, S.n Juan, y varios Ranchos de
numerosos Vecindarios en los margenes de los
Rios Conchos, Florido, y el de S.n Pedro por aver-
les acabado todos los bienes, y à muchos tambien las Vidas. El Valle de S.n Nicolas se avia
despoblado assi mismo de las dos partes de su
vecindario, y se disponia à hacer lo proprio la
tercera parte que quedaba por el justo temor de
perderlo todo.

16.   Estos males transcendieron hasta el Valle
de S.n Bartholomé, que dista de la Villa de Chiguagua sesenta leguas. Estube en el quando hize
mi entrada à las Provincias internas, y en la
Hacienda de S.ta Cruz de los Neyras me asegu-
ró su dueño aver ya acabado los Enemigos
con todos los bienes de Campo, reduciendo lo
poquissimo que le avia quedado al recinto de
su Casa por tenerlo seguro. Estendieronse tambien al Real del Parral, que dista de la Villa

setenta leguas. A la Hacienda Apantita, y Pueblo de Mapimí, cercana aquella al Presidio reformado de el Gallo, en donde el dia 30. de Agosto de el citado año de 71. mataron cinco personas; y aun hasta el Rio de Nasas, llevandose de la Hacienda de Sn Salvador de Orta toda la cavallada, y mas de trescientos cavallos con muerte de cinco Sirvientes; pero era objeto de maior compasion las muchas personas que han perdido repentinamente las vidas à la crueldad delos Barbaros, sin perdonar sexo, ni edad, pues despedazaban las criaturas en los pechos de sus Madres, y aun en sus vientres, executando en los difuntos Cuerpos los mas detestables excesos de la ferocidad, y sevicia: esto era un suficiente motivo que excitaba el christiano zelo de S. Exca à vindicar su justicia, con el merecido castigo de tan graves delitos.

17.   En los años de 7o. y 71. en la Hacienda del Mayorazgo, dieron muerte à mas de treinta personas; destrozaron notablemente el Ganado menor; llevandose toda la Cavallada, y Mulada, que encontraban; por lo que despoblada ya la Hacienda se retiró el Mayorazgo al Parral, quedando bastantemente empeñada esta familia. Y igual numero de muertes hicieron en el parage nombrado el Durazno cerca del Rio de Conchos. En la cañada de Cusiguriachi dieron muerte à cinco Harrieros de una Re-

cua que iba deesta Ciudad cargada de Generos, tomandose gran parte de ellos, y de las Mulas de Carga. En el Presidio de Janos fueron muertos por un ventajoso numero de Barbaros once Soldados, y cinco Yndios amigos, arrebatandoles mas de quinientos Cavallos dela guarnicion. Dela Hacienda de Dolores, perteneciente à Temporalidades, y de algunos vecinos, se llevaron mas de mil Caberas de Cavallada, y Mulada. Una legua distante dela Villa de Chiguagua en la Hacienda de Tabalaopa tambien de las Temporalidades mataron seis personas, y como doscientas Caberas de Ganado menor, por hacer daño hasta en lo que tienen algun provecho. En la Cañada de Tugo dos leguas dela Villa quitaron la vida à cinco personas. Immediatamente pasaron à la Hacienda de Bachimba, y executaron lo proprio con otras siete, no hallando oposicion en sus fuerzas. Despues dieron sobre la Hacienda de Sn Antonio dela Tavonera, en donde cruelmente mataron à diez y siete personas entre hombres, Mugeres, y Niños, dexandola totalmte despoblada. De alli fueron al Camino Real de Mexico, y dieron golpe à un Cordon de veinte, y uno Atajos de Mulas cargadas de Generos de varios interesados, y con ellos el Tavaco para el Rl Estanco: de noventa hombres entre dueños, Escolteros, y Harrieros que conducian esta Carga murieron siete, y los demas

huvieron de mirarse temerosos de la multitud
ventajosa de sus Enemigos: apoderados estos
de todo abrieron mas de ciento, y setenta ter-
cios de Ropa, Tavaco, y otros efectos, resultando de semejante destrozo un considerable es-
trago, pues aviendo cargado con lo que les
agrado, fueron desparramando en siete leguas
de distancia lo demas; de modo que reconoci-
do despues el daño con la total falta de Mulada, Sillas, y Aparejos, paró de treinta mil
pesos la perdida.

18.   En distinta ocasion asaltaron al Cordon
del Nuevo Mexico, como dos leguas dela
Villa, llevandose entonces como mil Bestias
Cavallares, y Mulares, despues de dexar sin
vida à siete personas. A su regresso le atacó
segunda vez tanto numero de Yndios, que siendo los nuestros como trescientos, y veinte
hombres, y despues de seis horas de una viva
resistencia, solo consiguieron matar tres Yndios,
herir à dos, y quitarles las partidas de Cavallos,
y Mulas, que encaminaban à sus tierras. You
al multitud de Barbaros aparecio en el
Rancho del Potrero, en el que no dexaron
persona con vida, aviendo perecido en este
general rebato tres Niños, y seis Niñas, de
cuias Criaturas la maior era de siete años,
y la menor de quatro meses, circunstancia
que demuestra bastantemente la ferocidad

de los Yndios, pues no perdonan aun á la inocen
cia mas indefensa. No descansa en esto su tira
nia, sino que se estiende á las mugeres embara
zadas abriendoles con el maior rigor los Vientres,
cuias inhumanidades no pueden ciertamente
referirse, sin ofensa del pudor, y honestidad.

19.	En el camino supe que el dia 11. de Octubre
de el mismo año se avian arrebatado de las cer
canias de la Villa de Chiguagua, y Real de
Santa Eulalia, como seiscientas Bestias cava
llares, y Mulares; muerto diez hombres de
catorce que salieron en su seguimiento; y heri
do aunque levemente á dn. Bernardo de Galvez
cinco Yndios enemigos, á quienes encontró avi
endo salido á alcanzar la Escuadra.

20.	Pocos dias antes de mi llegada dieron se
gundo golpe, llevandose los Cavallos, y Mulas
que avian quedado á los Mineros. Salio en su
alcance dn. Bernardo de Galvez con ciento, y vein
te y cinco Soldados de Cuera, y ciento y cin
cuenta Yndios de la Nacion Opata, y otros
amigos, el Capitan de Tulimes dn. Manuel
Muñoz, y el de Sn. Buenaventura dn. Nicolas
Gil: volvio dho Comandante con quarenta y cinco
hombres, y prosiguieron los otros sobre la huella
de los enemigos, pero sin conseguir el efecto de
sus fatigas.

21.	Despues de mi llegada á la Villa de Chiguagua,
y antes de tomar el mando de sus Fronteras

por los motivos que expuse al Exmo. S.r Virrey en Cartas de 22. de Noviembre, y 13. de Diciem.e de el año de 71. mataron en el camino de Tanos à un sobrino de el Capitan de el mismo Presidio, y dos Soldados que venian por medicamentos para el Capitan enfermo, que murio, como di cuenta à S. Exca. De la Hacienda de la Natividad de d.n Luis de Ylibarri se llevaron toda la Cavallada, y Mulada, practicando lo mismo en aquellos dias en el Valle de San Bartholomé, donde mataron à un Harriero, y se llevaron à un mancebo; que con otros tres que igualmente hirieron conducian unas cargas de Trigo à la Villa. En las Orillas de el Rio de S.n Pedro dieron muerte à siete Yndios Pescadores. De el Rio de Conchos se me participó aver dado un Yndio espia de los enemigos cinco lanzadas à otro de el Pueblo, quien murió à las tres horas recibidos los Santos Sacramentos. Otras tres personas huvo noticia avian muerto à manos de estos Barbaros cerca del Real de Cusiguriachi; de suerte que à los quince dias de mi entrada en la Villa, fuera de los robos, contaba yá no pocas muertes.

22.   Seria alargar demaciado este papel repetir los innumerables hechos publicos, y notorios de esta naturaleza en todas las Poblaciones, Haciendas, Ranchos, y caminos de la Provincia de la nueva Vizcaya, y solo hé particularizado alg.os

como por exemplares de lo que se experimentaba p.ª que se pueda formar una idea positiva de las muchas fatalidades que han padecido los habitadores de aquellos terrenos por las crueldades, muertes, y robos quasi diarios, que ya en unas, ya en otras partes practicaban los Barbaros, con mui poco detrimento de sus Esquadras.

23.   Entendido el abandono de Poblaciones enteras; el despueble de Haciendas, y Ranchos; el destrozo de las Cavalladas, Muladas, Ganados maiores, y menores; las repetidas muertes de Soldados, Vecinos, Pasageros, y gente de servicio; la perdida de bienes de todos; y la actual aniquilacion de los caudales de muchos, pues desde el mes de Enero del citado año de 71. hasta 20. de Diciembre del mismo solamente se contaban ciento y cincuenta muertos; diez y seis que escaparon heridos; otros tantos cautivos, y siete mil Bestias cavallares, y mulares robadas, fuera de los Ganados destrozados: y haciendo computo en el tiempo de la Guerra, segun juicio prudente de las personas mas reflexivas pasaban de quatro mil los que avian muerto de uno, y otro sexo, à manos de los Barbaros, y se numeraba la perdida de todos los efectos en mas de doce millones; se inferirà claramente el estado en que se hallaba la Provincia de la Viscaya; el descaecimiento de su Comercio, por no atreberse los interesados à remitir sus efectos, temiendo prudentemente su perdida, ni los dueños de Recuas à introducirlos con igual recelo de las de sus vidas, y

Mutiladas; la escasès de los bastimentos por la misma razon, y aun hasta deel carbon, y leña, por ser la gente que conducia esto, por mas desamparada, mas expuesta à perder sus vidas, como lo acreditan los repetidos exemplares.

24.   La decadencia delas Minas hà sido visible, y de bastante consideracion, pues siendo indispensable el uso de las Mulas para el beneficio de sus Metales, por no poderse acarrear de otro modo à las Haciendas, despedazarlos, ni molerlos se experimentaba grande atraso, assi en la conduccion de dichos Metales, è ingredientes para las revolturas, como en la de carbon para las fundiciones, y precisos bastimentos de los Operarios por la falta de Mulas, de suerte que à excepcion de una, ù otra Hacienda, que se hallaba con proporcion para tahona de agua, han parado las demas por los continuados robos de Bestias: causas todas que inspiraron las representaciones hechas al Govierno por los Diputados de aquella Mineria, y Comercio.

25.   No puedo omitir la importante reflexion de que esta Provincia tubo su principio el año de 7. de este siglo, hasta el de 48. corrieron solo 41. años, y en este corto tiempo logró tan conocidos aumentos en Villas, Reales de Minas, Pueblos, Valles, Haciendas, y otras menores Poblaciones, que hizo ventajosas respectivamente à todas las internas de este Reyno, contribuiendo à los

maiores creces del R.l Iterario; enriqueciendo
à muchos particulares; dando comodidades, y esperanzas de maiores intereses à sus habitadores; es-
tendiendo su comercio hasta esta Ciudad, y las
mas principales del Reyno, y dando principio à
muchos caudales en las Provincias internas: motivos estos para que fuesse su Poblacion la mas
numerosa, convocada de sus riquezas, y sin gastos
del Rey nuestro Señor. Pero aunque comenzó
la Guerra el año de 48. hasta el dia 2.o de Diciembre de el de 71. con continuado teson por veinte y tres años, para el curso de las indicadas
felicidades, dando causa à sus conocidos atrasos.
Existen las mismas Minas que comenzaron, por
lograr este terreno la ventajosa circunstancia de no
aguarse alguna. Entre ellas ai muchas de Oro, y
Plata que ofrecen grandes riquezas, y se desfruc-
tarían con abundancia, si las gentes que ai, y pudieran congregarse lograssen vivir con desago,
y trabajar sin el imminente riesgo de perder sus
bienes, y vidas en las continuas irrupciones de
los Barbaros.

27.   Prueba esta verdad el haver en la Villa de
Chiguagua Mineros que llegaron à hacer re-
mesa hasta de cien Barras de Plata: y en el
año de 71. fue tan escaso el despacho que salio
de alli, que huvo entre aquellos quien no pudiesse despachar una. Sin embargo de esta notable diferencia, vinieron à esta Capital seisci-

entas, y ocho Barras, se lo que se infiere que la Provincia de la Vizcaya libre de las hostilidades de tan continuada, y cruda Guerra, como ha padecido, y que otra no huviera sufrido tanto tiempo sin llegar al termino de su total destruccion, no solo es bastante à enriquecerse asi misma, y hacer felices à sus habitadores con lo que puede producir, sino aumentar el Comercio de todo el Reyno con visibles utilidades de la Real Hacienda en las Alcavalas, Quintos, Ensayes, y demas justas contribuciones.

28.   Tampoco puedo dexar de advertir ser esta Provincia paso al Comercio, y comunicacion con el nuevo Mexico, y las de Sonora, Tarahumara, Sinaloa, Nayarit, Pimerias Alta, y Baxa con muchas Poblaciones, Presidios, y Misiones en que se trataba de la conversion de numerosas Naciones; y haciendose con el tiempo, y la introduccion de los Barbaros, y su despueble intrasitables los caminos, seria preciso ò que todo se perdiesse, ò abandonasse, ò que para el remedio fuessen indispensables crecidos gastos.

29.   En la Villa de Chiguagua se mantenia una compañia de sesenta Soldados de Cuera; veinte y cinco Indios Norteños, y veinte y uno Tanchez. los primeros con veinte pesos mensales de paga cada uno, y los otros con

diez. Quarenta, y un hombres incluso el Capitan Theniente, Alferes, Sargento, y quatro cabos de Esquadra en el Presidio de Cerro Gordo, distante de la Villa de Chiguagua, y rumbo al Sur, como cien leguas. Quarenta hombres inclusos los Oficiales en el Presidio de Guaxuquilla, distante de la Villa, y por el mismo rumbo que el antecedente sesenta leguas. Cincuenta hombres comprehendidos los Oficiales en el Presidio de Julimes veinte y dos leguas de la Villa. Cincuenta hombres en el Presidio de S.n Buenaventura, distante sesenta leguas rumbo al Norte. Y cincuenta en el de Janos distante noventa, y cinco leguas por el mismo rumbo. Con que se hallaban en esta basta Provincia trescientos treinta y siete Soldados entre los Destacamentos de Presidios, los de Cuera, é Indios de la Nacion Norteña, y Tanche.

30. Para formar un cuerpo de Tropa en las campañas que se hicieron fue preciso desmembrar los expresados Presidios, sacando Esquadras de todos. A estos se agregaron los Indios de la Nacion Opata, y otras amigos, con que ascendian al numero de trescientos, y mas hombres, à excepcion de la primera Campaña hecha por d.n Lope de Cuellar, que llegó à setecientos por aver tenido orden de levantar un Cuerpo de Reclutas, que luego se reformó, y segun entiendo sin orden, ni providencia de este Superior Govierno, ni tampoco con anuencia del

Ilmo Sor dn Joseph de Galvez, à cuias superiores ordenes eraba el mencionado Cuellar.

31. En el tiempo que duró la primera Campaña que hizo dn Lope de Cuellar, dieron golpe los Yndios en el Pueblo de Sn Geronimo, distante cinco leguas dela Villa de Chiguagua, matando quarenta y nueve Personas entre hombres, mugeres, y niños, y cautivando once. A los tres dias lo dieron en la Mision de el Nombre de Dios una legua de dicha Villa, pereciendo ocho individuos à sus infames manos.

32. En la segunda asaltaron la Hacienda de la Tavonera, en la que apenas quedó tal qual con vida. Immediatamente en el camino Rl. destrozaron veinte, y un Atajo de Fardería de el Comercio con muerte de siete de los Conductores, y perdida dela Mulada.

33. En la tercera dieron en el Valle de Sn Bartholomé, y Hacienda de Bachimbo, resultando once personas muertas, y diez cautivas, à mas de tres mil, y tantas Bestias Cavallares, y Mulares que se llevaron.

34. En la quarta campaña que salio el dia 6. de Septiembre de 71. y volvio el 28. de Octubre de el mismo hicieron veinte y ocho muertes, hizieron à varios, y se llevaron mas de mil y setecientas Bestias: y repitiendo segunda entrada, cargaron con la Mulada que avia quedado à los Mineros, motivo por que cessasse el trabajo

[18]

de las mas Haciendas de Plata con notable atraso de sus dueños, y de el Común.

35. De todo lo hasta aqui expresado se conoce à todas luces, que con los doscientos noventa y un hombres de Tropa que avia existentes en la Provincia no se podian evitar los robos, muertes, y destrozos de los Enemigos; contenerlos en sus continuas entradas; ni escarmentarlos con el justo castigo que merecian su altivez, osadia, y crueldad.

36. Al logro de tan importante objeto se dedicó d.ⁿ Bernardo de Galvez en el corto tiempo que fue Comandante de la Frontera, no perdonando este animoso Oficial fatigas, desvelos, ni riesgos, que pudiessen conducir à la consecucion de sus loables designios, dando exemplo à su Tropa en el valor, y en la constancia que requiere tan extraña guerra como lo testifica el hecho de haver dicho Oficial recibido varias heridas en las distintas funciones que tubo con los Enemigos.

37. La Provincia de Coahuila, segun informes de su Governador se hallaba hostilizada por los Apaches Mescaleros, y en su Frontera el Presidio de S.ⁿ Juan Baptista de el Rio Grande deel Norte, Monclova, S.ᵗᵃ Rosa del Sacramento, y el de S.ⁿ Saba, que por providencia de el Govierno se destinó à la Villa de S.ⁿ Fernando de Austria, con calidad de hasta nueva Orden: y aunque con esta fuerza se podia aver contenido el orgullo delos Mezcaleros, no se ha verificado por la vergonzosa in—

accion de esta Tropa, que conocio bien el Exmo

Sor Marquès de Rubi, y lo expreso en la nota

que se halla en su Dictamen General, dando el

epiteto de emmohecidas à las Armas de esta

Provincia, para manifestar el poco uso que de

ellas se hacia.

38.   De Sonora eran frecuentes los avisos de

las hostilidades que en su Frontera cometian

los Apaches, domiciliados en la intrincada, y

dilatada Sierra de Chiricagui, y para liber-

tarse de estos daños se hallaba con los Presidios

siguientes: Fronteras, Terrenate, Tubac, Sta

Gertrudis de el Altar, Sn Miguel de Orcasitas,

Buena vista, y una Compañia Volante. La gu-

arnicion de cada uno de sus Presidios constaba

de un Capitan, Theniente, Alferez, Sargento, qua-

tro Cabos, y quarenta, y dos Soldados de Cuera;

pero esta ultima no tenia Oficiales, por estar

agregada al Presidio de Terrenate, y à las orde-

nes de su Capitan dn Joseph Antonio de Vildo-

sola.

39.   En la Nueva Mexico hacian sus irrupciones

los Cumanches por el rumbo de el Norte, y por

el de el Poniente los Apaches Gileños. En dicha Pro-

vincia ai un Presidio de ochenta hombres in-

cluso el Capitan, que lo es el Governador de ella,

dos Thenientes, un Alferez, y dos Sargentos, y

un numeroso vecindario capaz de defenderse

por si mismo, assi por su multitud, como por

su acreditado espíritu militar, y valor que asiste à sus individuos.

40.   La Provincia delos Texas se hallaba con los Presidios nombrados N. S. del Pilar delos Adaes con sesenta hombres incluso los Oficiales; S.ⁿ Agustin de Ahumada con treinta y un hombres inclusos el Capitan, un Theniente, y un Sargento. La Bahia de el Espiritu Santo con cincuenta hombres comprehendidos el Capitan, Theniente, Alferez, y un Sargento: y con el de S.ⁿ Antonio de Bexar, cuia dotacion se componia de Capitan, Sargento, dos Cavos, y diez y nueve Soldados de Cuera. Sin embargo sus terrenos eran continuamente insultados por las belicosas, y numerosas Naciones del Norte, de cuio numero, y circunstancias hablaré en el lugar que corresponde, como assi mismo de los vastos terrenos que compone esta hermosa presea).

41.   Atendiendo el Govierno á los fundados, y repetidos informes sobre las hostilidades que diariam.^{te} cometian las Naciones indicadas de el Norte en las immediaciones de el Presidio de S.ⁿ Antonio de Bexar, Villa de S.ⁿ Fernando, y las cinco opulentas Misiones que en la corta distancia de tres leguas se hallan establecidas en el Rio de San Antonio, se resolvio por Decreto expedido en el mes de febrero, ó Marzo de el año pasado de 70. la translacion de el Presidio de S.ⁿ Agustin de Ahumada al de S.ⁿ Antonio de Bexar, reforzando aquella Guarnicion con un Theniente, y

veinte Soldados del de S.n Saba, para que con
estas fuerzas, y con el auxilio de los Indios de
las Misiones, tubiesse el Governador no solo la
suficiente à impedir las hostilidades que los Enemigos cometían en los Terrenos immediatos;
vino tambien la mui competente para seguir,
y castigarlos en sus proprias Rancherias, y so
le remitieron para su logro algunos Fusiles, y
munisiones de Guerra, aunque segun tengo
entendido aprovecharon poco estas providencias, por el ningun uso que de ellas se hizo.

42.   El Exmo Sor Marqués de Rubi en su dis-
creto dictamen que hallará V.S. en el Archivo
de Chiguagua describe con bastante propriedad,
y acierto la poca, ò ninguna utilidad que experimentaba el Servicio en la antigua situacion
delos Presidios, el Govierno interior de estos, y
el perverso dolo con que se manejaba el triste Sueldo de el soldado: señala las alturas en que
se hallaban los Presidios, y todo lo demas que
expone en sus Revistas hace conocer la variacion que se requeria: por lo que tengo por ocioso difundirme, quando mas bien de èl que de
mis experiencias puede deducirse el acierto con
que se formò la nueva R.l Instruccion por
que se goviernan las Tropas, y Presidios de el
mando de V.S.

43.   Este era el estado en que Yo hallé las Provincias internas quando tomé el mando de

ellas, y creido de aver satisfecho plenamente al primer punto dela Carta de V.S. de 17. de Mayo, referiré ahora las providencias que consecuentem.te se dictaron en vista de mis informes, bien que con el recelo de olvidar algunas esenciales por existir en Chiguagua todos los documentos que las contienen, y ser preciso apelar à la memoria.

Providencias de la Junta de Guerra, y Real Hacienda de 2. de Abril de 1772. ||

44. Siempre consideré Yo que las tristes noticias de tantos males sorprenderian el animo de el Sor Virrey dedicado à hacer felices aquellas Provincias; y que sin tomar algunas resoluciones mui seguras, y prontas no podria conseguirse el fin, arriesgando el Rey lo que avia quedado en ellas. Con efecto de comun acuerdo se resolvio en la citada Junta la translacion de los Presidios de Julimes, Cerro gordo, Sn Saba, Sta Rosa, y Monclova. El primero à la Junta de los Rios Norte, y Conchos, cuio nombre tiene àhora, y en donde antes estaba establecido: y los otros quatro à las Orillas del Rio grande del Norte en todo el Terreno que ai como de ciento y quarenta leguas desde aquel hasta el de Sn Juan Baptista, à fin de cubrir las Fronteras de las Provincias de la Nueva Vizcaya y Coahuila, segun tambien estaba determinado en el nuevo proyecto, y Reglamento de situacion de Presidios en la linea. Dieronseme las corres-

pondientes Ordenes para que reconocidos por
los Governadores de estas Provincias con proligidad los parages llanos, fertiles, y mas ápropo-
sito se situaran los Presidios á distancias iguales, ô proporcionadas, practicando las demas di-
ligencias, y reconocimientos, que para el nuevo
establecimiento de los quatro Presidios removentes se prevenia en los Capitulos 19. 20. 21. y 22.
de dicho Reglamento.

45.   Remitieronsenos copias para nuestra
instruccion, y govierno, con prevencion de que
si por ausencia, ô legitimo impedimento de los
Governadores de Coahuila, y Nueva Vizcaya
no pudiessen estos concurrir al reconocimiento
de los parages mas cercanos á aquellos Govier-
nos en que debian situarse los quatro Presidios
trasladables, lo executasse por mi mismo, ô
por personas inteligentes que Yo comisiona-
sse al efecto.

46.   Que se asignasse, y librassen, como se prevenia en el yá citado Reglamento, á favor de los
Capitanes de los cinco Presidios transmigrables
la cantidad de tres mil pesos para costear la
nueva construccion del recinto que debe ocupar cada uno en el parage que se les señala-
ra, en el qual para que la fabrica fuesse con
arreglo al nuevo Plan, se avia de formar primero el Quadro de Tapias comunes de adoves,
y los dos pequeños Baluartes en sus angulos

levantando despues en lo interior de la Capilla, Cuerpo de Guardia, Casa de el Capitan, y habitacio-
nes de los Soldados, è Indios amigos, y Exploradores, guarneciendose todos entretanto en Tiendas
de Campaña, y Barracas provisionales, y la entrega de dichos tres mil pesos se mandò à Oficiales
Reales de esta Capital la executassen à los Apoderados, y Haviadores que los Capitanes de dichos
Presidios tenian en ella, baxo de la acostumbra-
da fianza de presentar la cuenta respectiva de
su distribucion.

47.　　Que en el caso de que en los parages donde entonces se hallaban los Presidios que debian trasladarse quedassen las familias, y vecindario que avia
en ellos, subsistiessen para su resguardo, y defenza
las fortificaciones materiales que tenian; y en el
de que se trasladassen tambien con la Tropa de
dhos Presidios à sus nuevas situaciones, se demo-
lieran arrazandolas enteramente para evitar
que usassen de ellas los Enemigos en qualquiera
encuentro, ò seguimiento que contra ellos hiciessen nuestras Tropas.

48.　　Que al Presidio de Sn Antonio de Bexar se aumentasse su guarnicion, como se proponia en el nuevo reglamento, hasta el numero de ochenta plazas, com
puestas de un Capitan, dos Thenientes, un Alferez,
un Capellan, dos Sargentos, y setenta y tres Cabos,
y Soldados, pero con el goze de los actuales sueldos,
que entonces tenian los Oficiales, y demas individuos

de aquel Presidio.

4º.   Que no solo se aumentasse la Compañia de sesenta hombres de Chiguagua hasta el numero de ciento, sino que tambien se levantassen otras tres de igual numero de Gente de el Pais, como se proponia, para que la primera con los quarenta y cinco Indios amigos exploradores, que actualmente tenia, se empleasse en contener los insultos de los enemigos en los caminos, y Haciendas de labor, para que con este auxilio se trabaxassen las Minas de el Real de Sta. Eulalia, y pudieran beneficiarse con algun desaogo sus Platas en las Haciendas immediatas à dicha Villa; y las otras tres sirviessen para el mismo fin, quando la necesidad lo exigiesse, y mas principalmente para expeler los Enemigos de el parage de el Agua nueva, y demas à que tambien fuesse necesario destinarlas à maiores distancias: y assi mismo para que al tiempo de trasladarse à sus nuevas situaciones los referidos Presidios recorriessen, y guardassen el largo terreno intermedio que avia desde los parages en que estaban, hasta los que debian ocupar, à fin de que no quedaran los enemigos à espaldas de ellos, y los arrojasse à la otra parte de el Rio grande de el Norte, sin consentir por ningun pretexto que los Apaches Lipanes quedassen en el distrcito de Coahuila.

50. Que las quatro compañias Volantes de cien hombres, se compusieran de un Capitan, con el sueldo de cien pesos al mes; de dos Thenientes, con el de cincuenta; dos Alfereses con quarenta; dos Sargentos, con veinte y quatro; quatro Cabos, con veinte y dos; y ochenta y nueve Soldados, con veinte pesos cada uno.

51. Que à cada una de las tres, que nuevamente debian formarse, se agregassen veinte y cinco Yndios amigos exploradores, con el sueldo de tres reales diarios, quedando en la de Chiguagua los quarenta y cinco que tenia, con el sueldo que hasta alli gozaban.

52. Que se nombrassen dos Ayudantes Mayores para las funciones de su oficio, en las partes en que se dividian, y destinassen dichas Compañias con el sueldo de cincuenta y cinco pesos al mes cada uno, de los quales debian costear el Armamento de Escopetas, Lanzas, Adargas, y Cueras, dandoles de cuenta de el Rey los seis Cavallos, y una Mula que por las antiguas Ordenanzas de Presidios estaba prevenido para cada uno, por no poder soportar su costo de su sueldo, por el crecido que tienen en aquellos Paises las Armas, y Generos para vestuario.

53. Que debiendo ser los Oficiales, y Ayudantes Mayores de aquellas quatro Compañias Volantes sugetos de valor, aptitud, y experiencia de el modo de guerrear los Yndios enemigos, y conocimiento

de sus maximas, y astucias, y parages en que suelen emboscarse, y acoerse, se propusiessen por mi à esta Capitania General aquellos que consideraba mas aproposito, cuidando igualm.te de que los Reclutas que se hiciessen para la formacion de ellas, fuessen tambien gentes utiles, y esforzadas, y que tubiessen conocimiento de los terrenos, è Indios enemigos, para que fuesse el servicio con honor de la nacion, y utilidad de el Estado.

54.	Que en el interin que S. M. determinaba sobre la formacion de la linea de Presidios, proyectada por el Exmo Sor Marqués de Rubi, y Nombramiento de Oficiales Generales, è Inspector que previene el Reglamento formado en tiempo de el S.or Marqués de Croix, para el govierno de los Presidios situados en linea, seme nombrasse por Comandante General de las Tropas de Chiguagua, y demas de las Fronteras: y en consideracion al trabaxo, y gastos en los Viages, y Campañas, seme asignò la gratificacion de dos mil pesos anuales, sobre el sueldo de seiscientos que gozaba, como Capitan de el Presidio de S.n Saboo.

55.	En atencion à que en el estado que remiti con carta de 18 de febrero de el numero de gentes de que se componia la compañia de Chigua. gua, expresè estar sin Armamento la Tropa que actualmente tenia, lo que arguia inopia de Armas: se remitieron prontamente quinientas cincuenta Carabinas, ò Escopetas proprias de Cavalleria, y otras tantas Espadas con sus Rainas, y el numero de piedras, y balas que se considerò bastante, para que hiciessen el servicio en el tiempo de un año, no solo esta Compañia, sino tambien las tres de cien hombres que debian formarse, y por la Real Factoria seme pasò razon de el valor de dichas Armas, Piedras, y Balas, con noticia de el flete de ellas, para que repartiendose entre los individuos de las quatro Compañias, se les descontasse su monto de sus respectivos sueldos, por deberlo estos soportar, previniendoseme tambien, que en caso de que los Yndios amigos, y Exploradores no usassen de Escopetas, y Espadas, y si de Lanzas, ò Chuzos, se vendiessen las sobrantes de cuenta de la R.l Hacienda à los vecinos de Chiguagua que quisieran comprarlas para su uso, y defensa de sus Casas, y Haciendas.

56. Atento à que de cuenta de S. M. se daban seis libras de Polvora cada año à los Soldados de los Presidios internos para sus exercicios, y funciones Militares contra los Barbaros, se mandò proveerles con igual numero de libras à cada individuo de las quatro Compañias Volantes, y que el monto de los habilitados se remitiesse con prontitud de cuenta de S. M. y q.e en el interin llegaba à aquella Villa, se submi-

nistrara de la R.l Factoria la que se necesitaba para dicha Tropa con calidad de reinte-
grarla à la Administracion de este Ramo el
costo principal, y fletes hasta Chiguagua.

57.   Que para los pagamentos de dichas quatro Compañias, è Indios amigos agregados à
ellas, y sueldos de el Comandante General, se remitiesse à principios de cada año el caudal competente : se aplicassen los cinco mil pesos q.e
restaban por pagarse en quatro años delos veinte y cinco mil dela redencion del Presidio de
el Pasage, y lo sobrante en cada año delos presidios, y arbitrios dela Villa de Chiguagua, como tambien el monto de los granos de Plata
con que contribuie aquella Mineria; todo lo
qual ascendia à doce mil pesos anuales.

58   Que para subvenir con prontitud à los pagamentos de Tropa en el citado primero año
de 72. y compra de Cavallos, y Mulas con que
debian ser proveidos, se diesse por el Exmo
S.or Virrey la Orden correspondiente al Yn-
tendente dela Sonora d.n Pedro Corbalan para
que remitiera sin perder instante, y con competente Escolta para su segura conduccion los
cien mil pesos en moneda, que se embiaron
dela Caxas de esta Capital à aquella Provincia,
y tenia avisado se hallaban detenidos en el
Real del Pitic, por no poderse emplear en el rescate
de Plata, y Oro pasta à que fueron destinados.

59.   Que siendo preciso que en la Villa de Chiguagua
huviesse sugeto que hiciera las funciones de Comisario, y Thesorero de Guerra, y pasasse las revistas mensales à las quatro Compañias de cien
hombres, è Indios agregados à ellas, y que con
arreglo à los estractos de las Revistas, formaliza-
sse este los ajustes de sus sueldos, pagando men-
salmente, ò cada tercio de año el monto de ellos, se
pusiesse por mi sugeto aproposito para todo,
que llevara formales cuentas, con la precision
de presentarlas al Real Tribunal de ellas en sus
debidos tiempos, y desde luego sele asignaron
dos mil pesos de sueldo para si, y quatrocientos
para un Escribiente que le ayudasse, afianzando
previamente hasta la cantidad de diez mil pesos.

60.   Que en el interin se nombraba sugeto que sir-
viesse este empleo pasasse las revistas mensales à las Tropas de Chiguagua el Corregidor
de aquella Villa, en las quales interviniesse su
Comandante, y por enfermedad, ò ausencia de este
el Capitan, ù Oficial de maior graduacion de dicha
Tropa, y con arreglo à las expresadas Revistas
se hiciessen los pagamentos en moneda, conforme à los Sueldos señalados para que de este modo pudiesse disfrutarlos la Tropa, comprando
con ella lo que necesitaba, y para que tambien
sele hiciera los descuentos respectivos del monto
de el Armamento, que debia recibir de cuenta de
el Rey.

61. Que consultando al ahorro de la R.l Hacienda, se facilitasse de el monto de los anuales situados de los quatro Presidios nombrados de
los Adaes, S.n Agustin de Ahumada, Monterrey, y Mesa del Tonati en el Nayarit,
que por el nuevo reglamento se mandaban extinguir, teniendo consideracion à que impor-
tando el todo la cantidad de sesenta, y quatro
mil, doscientos ocho pesos, y tomines, podia
subvenirse con ella en mucha parte à los crecidos gastos que debian erogar las providencias
indicadas: pero teniendola tambien à las frecuentes noticias de los estragos, muertes, y robos, que los Apaches continuaban en todas
partes, y à que podria franquear à estos mas
campo, y libertad para sus irrupciones la extincion de dichos quatro Presidios, al paso q.e
se podia evitar que sucediesse; se me dio orn
para que bien instruido de la subsistencia de
dichos Presidios en la actual situacion, y de
la de los Paises insultados por los Indios, in-
formasse si convendria que se mantubiessen
en los parages en que estaban ubicados, ò q.e
se extinguiessen todos, ò alguno de ellos, mas
que si consideraba precisa su subsistencia para
hacer mas bien la guerra por todas partes à los Barbaros, no practicasse novedad
en ellos.

62. Que en el caso de considerar precisa la ex-

extinción de los Presidios delos Adaes, S.ⁿ Agus-tin de Ahumada, y Monterrey, debia executarse prontamente, manteniendose en el primero su Gover-nador con el sueldo que le estaba asignado para que pudiesse administrar justicia en la Provincia; y si el segundo se practicasse otro tanto, pero siendolo tam-bien la extinción del de Monterrey, quedassen en él no obstante su Governador, y el Capellan con los Soldados de dotacion à mas de una Escuadra de ocho hombres con el sueldo cada uno de doscientos pesos anuales, que tambien prevenia el reglamento.

63.   Determinose tambien, que si parecia extin-guible el Presidio dela Mesa de el Tonati, me arre-glasse à lo prevenido por el citado reglamento, en que estaba mandado dexar siete Guardias con dos-cientos pesos cada uno al año, y un Oficial con ca-torce hombres dela Compañia de Voluntarios de Cataluña; con solo el sueldo militar que gozaba, bien que al Oficial Comandante sele asignaron sobre el suio quinientos pesos anuales en calidad de ayuda de costa.

Disposiciones dadas à consecuencia de lo resuelto en la citada Junta, y felices efectos q produxeron.

64.   Antes de recibir los ordenes de el Govierno, dese-oso à impulsos de mi zelo de precaver los daños que Chiguaga, y sus immediaciones experimenta-ban, me dediqué à emplear con prontitud la poca

Tropa que tenía: y practicado personal, y prolixamente el reconocimiento, y examen de aquellos terrenos dispuse con fecha de 2. de Junio de el año de 72. que las Escuadras de los Presidios de Cerro gordo, y Guaxuquilla fuessen de veinte hombres cada una con su Oficial: que las de la Villa de Chiguagua, assi como las de los Presidios de Julimes, Sn Buenaventura, Janos, y Paso de el Norte se compusieran de veinte y cinco plazas, y su respectivo Oficial; y à unos, y otros señalé los terrenos, rumbos, y parages que debían cortar, y vigilar. Se continuo en el modo siguiente:

Presidio de Cerro gordo.

65.	La Escuadra de este Presidio cortaba Arroyo abaxo hasta donde basua por Sn Bernardo, Sn Blas, Barrasa, y de alli à los Reyes, de donde se volvia por los mismos parages al Presidio.

Presidio de Guaxuquilla.

66.	La Escuadra de este Presidio cortaba saliendo por los Chupaderos al Carrisalillo: de alli se tiraba à Julimes, ó al Rincon de Carros, de donde se regresaba al Presidio sobre su misma huella.

Presidio de Julimes.

67.   La Escuadra de este Presidio cortaba saliendo por el paso de el Cholomè al Potrero de la Herran, hasta Hormigas, de donde se regresaba à su Presidio.

Villa de Chiguagua.

68.   La primera Escuadra cortaba por el Palo Blanco, al Venado, los Reyes, y el Barrigon, en donde esperaba la segunda, que cortaba por Jesus Maria, la Cueva, Maxalca, Victorino, el Potrero, cogiendo la orilla de la Sierra hasta la cañada de la Noria, la que reoxis traba siguiendo su derrota por la Laguna de San Martin hasta el Barrigon, en donde se juntaba con la primera; y dandose los Oficiales certificacio-nes uno à otro firmadas de dos testigos de averse juntado en dicho parage, se regresaban à la Villa por los mismos rumbos que avian llevado.

Presidio de Sn. Buenaventura.

69.   La Escuadra de este Presidio cortaba saliendo por el Alamo à la Noria, à lo de Ruiz, por lo de Velarde al Vado de el Rio de Santa Maria, en donde se juntaba con la Escuadra de Janos, pa-sando ambas à las Salinas, de donde se regresaba por los mismos parages al Presidio.

Presidio de Janos.

70. La Escuadra de este Presidio cortaba saliendo por la Estancia delos Nogales al vado de el Rio de Santa Maria, en donde se juntaban con la Escuadra de S.n Buenaventura, y corriendo ambas unidas hasta las Salinas, se regresaba por los mismos parages à su Presidio.

Presidio de el Paso.

71. La Escuadra de este Presidio cortaba por el ojito de Samalayuca hasta las Salinas, en donde hallaria, ò esperaria las Escuadras de Janos, y S.n Buenaventura, y dandose mutuamente los tres Oficiales Certificaciones de averse juntado en dicho parage en la indicada forma se regresaban por los mismos parages à sus Presidios

72. Previnose à todas las referidas Escuadras estubiessen fuera delos Presidios empleadas en cortar, y revisar los terrenos que à cada una se asignaba segun el Plan expresado, por el tiempo de quince dias.

73. Que por ningun motivo variassen sus destinos, y rumbos, sino solo en el caso de encontrar alguna huella delos Enemigos, que entrara, ò saliesse, lo que siendo fresca, ò de poco tiempo debian seguirla, y si lograban alcanzarles, y hallaban no pasar los Barbaros de cien hombres, debian atacarles sin alguna detencion, salvo que pudiessen lograr sorprenderlos à la mañana siguiente.

74. Que si el numero delos Barbaros excediesse de cien hombres, y diessen tiempo por estar arranchados à que se juntasse con la Escuadra, ò Escuadras delos Presidios immediatos, se diesse el aviso correspondiente, supuesto que por el Derrotero asignado à cada Escuadra, podia hacerse cargo de las distancias, y parages en que podian hallarse.

75. Dispusose que en esta tan indispensable, como penosa fatiga alternassen los capitanes de los Presidios, y Villa de Chiguagua con los Thenientes, y Alfereces, saliendo cada uno quince dias con sus Escuadras, y à las veinte y quatro horas de aver llegado la una saliesse la otra, para lo qual debia estar dispuesta, y bastimentada al efecto, de modo que siembre se verificasse estar todas en un movimiento continuo.

76. A los Capitanes, y Subalternos se les constituio en la obligacion de formar un diario puntual de los acaecimientos mas principales en los quince dias, y delas funciones que lograban tener con los Enemigos, como era preciso muchas veces. En este caso debian notar puntualmente el parage; el numero de los muertos, y heridos; y el de las presas que hicieran de personas, y cavalladas, sin olvidar la descripcion dela perdida que se experimentara por nuestra parte, remitiendo estos Documentos cada mes à la Comandancia, para dar parte por ellos al Govierno, segun se ha practicado.

77.	En los Diarios, è informes originales, que se hallan en el Archivo de Chiguagua, se manifestan patentemente los efectos de estas disposiciones, y el crecido numero de cavallada, y mulada que pudo quitarse à los Indios, y restituirse à sus dueños, de cuia constancia testificarà el Thesorero dela Expedicion que llevò puntual cuenta, interin Yo pueda afirmar à V.S. que hasta entonces no avian sabido respirar de sus angustias los vecinos de Chiguagua, y sus immediaciones, por los insultos que les ocasionaban las muchas Rancherias de Indios domiciliados en las immediatas Sierras, en que se consiguio alexarlos à esfuerzos dela infatigable persecucion.

78.	Posteriormente se acordò en otras dos Juntas de Guerra, y R.l Hacienda el aumento dela Compañia de Chiguagua hasta el numero de cien hombres: el de otros trescientos que Yo tenia consultados; y para subvenir à los gastos dela expedicion se mandò remitir, y aplicar à ella los cien mil pesos que existian en el Pitic Provincia de Sonora.

79.	Dediqueme desde luego à la Recluta de los trescientos hombres, publicando Vando en Chiguagua, y en los Pueblos comarcanos para conseguirlo mas prontamente: destiné Oficiales à varias partes con el mismo oboeto, y por medio de aquel Corregidor, y demas Justicias solicité el auxilio de los veinte y cinco Indios que se resolvio agregar à cada Compañia, quedando en Chiguagua las quarenta y cinco que ya exis-tian.

80. Recultado, pues, el numero de hombres referido con la satisfaccion de sus circunstancias, y aptitud pa-ra la fatiga, di quantas providencias me parecieron con-ducentes à la compra de Cavalladas, y Mulladas, y me vi en la precision de apelar al Povernador dela Provin.ᵃ para facilitar mejor el exito, sin dexar de hacer iguales encargos à otras diferentes personas, que à distancias podian aprontar algunas, y entonces fue qu-ando el Administrador del Conde de S.ⁿ Pedro del Alamo ministrò quatrocientos setenta y dos Cava-llos en parte del pago de su debito.

81. Pasé al Povierno succesivamente las propuestas de Capitanes, y demàs Oficiales subalternos, y con-sulté para comisario, y Fhesorero dela Expedicion à d.ⁿ Manuel Antonio de Escorza, sugeto de las calidades necesarias al desempeño de tal cargo, y que se hallaba entonces separado enteramente del Comercio.

82. Procedi de acuerdo con el Intendente de Sonora d.ⁿ Pedro Corbalan à la segura conduccion, y recibo delos cien mil pesos existentes dela R.�l Hacienda, que se hallaban en el Pitic, facilitando Escoltas, y otros auxilios: y aviendo llegado à Chiguagua este caudal el dia 13. de Octubre, entrò desde luego en poder del Fhesorero Escorza, y se entregò tam

bien á este la distribucion: de los diez mil pesos q.
avian importado las pagas, y Pre de la Oficialidad,
y Tropa de la Compañia de chiguagua desde el dia
21. de Diciembre del año anterior de 74. en que
hizo la entrega d.ⁿ Bernardo de Galvez, hasta
el en que tomó posesion de ella su nuevo Capitan d.ⁿ Fran.ᶜᵒ de la Borbolla, acompañando
assi mismo las revistas mensales, que se le
avian pasado por el Corregidor.

83.   Remiti á los Capitanes de los Presidios removentes las Cartas Ordenes en que se les manda-
ba estar á las mias. Passé al Governador de la
Provincia de Sonora el correspondiente aviso p.ᵃ
que con conocimiento de las operaciones que me-
ditaba contra los Barbaros, y tiempos en que debian comenzarse, practicasse por si lo que debia:
y á los de Nueva Vizcaya, y Coahuila el en que
convenia practicar la translacion de los Presidios
de sus respectivas Provincias, que fue quanto por
entonces me parecio conveniente en cumplimiento
delas resoluciones dela Junta.

84.   Aviase tenido en ella presentes los fundamien-
tos, y razones con que el Exmo S.ᵒʳ Marques de
Rubi opinaba la extincion delos quatro Presidios
citados, y como por lo respectivo al delos Adaes
consulté Yo lo mismo quando estube de Govern.ᵒʳ
interino de la Provincia delos Texas, haciendo
presente su gravosa, é inutil existencia, en
cuio dictamen convino con migo el Gefe de Es-

cuadra d.n Antonio Ulloa reconocida su situacion, se
dexó à mi arbitrio la extincion, ò permanencia de
este, y los demas que existian, segun lo considerasse
conducente.

85.   Esta honrosa confianza, y el deseo de correspon-
derla me obligó à decir ingenuamente que el Presidio
de los Adaes sobre no contribuir à la defensa, no podia servir à la ofensa de los Apaches en las Fronteras
de Nueva Vizcaya, y Coahuila, ni menos à la de Texas à que tocaba por hallarse situado mas de trescientas leguas de el Rio de S.n Antonio de Bexar,
donde esta ubicado el de este nombre, y se hallan
la Villa de S.n Fernando con cinco Misiones, y
el de la Bahia de el Espiritu Santo con otras dos,
àmas de ser aquel terreno uno de los que nunca
han llegado à pisar los Indios Apaches Lipanes,
Naxages, y otros en tiempo de paz, ni guerra por
el impedimento de la distancia, y el de muchas numerosas Naciones barbaras, que son sus mortales
Enemigos.

86.   El conocimiento practico de el Terreno en que
existia el indicado Presidio sin Vecindarios, Pueblos,
ni Misiones que sostener, cuio objeto, y el de la
reduccion de Naciones Barbaras es siempre el con
que se establecen los fronterizos me executo à opinar assi agregando que de nada avia podido servir, ni serviria en lo succesivo que de demarcar, ò
separar la dominacion de el Rey nuestro Soberano
con la de S. M. Christianissima por lo respectivo

à la Provincia de la Luisiana; pero que aviendo cesado este motivo con la entrega de ella, y transferidose à S. M. la permanencia, no me parecia aver otro imaginable para la subsistencia de aquel Presidio.

87. Dixe tambien no ser conducente, ni util para la contencion de los Indios Barbaros de la Nacion Apache, ni para las operaciones ofensivas el de Monterrey en el Nuevo Reyno de Leon, fundandome en que este Presidio assi por la mucha distancia à que se halla de la Frontera de los enemigos, como por quedar yà en el centro de nuestras poblaciones Jamas hà empleado sus Armas contra dichas Naciones, ni aun en tiempo de la mas viva guerra en la Provincia de Texas, maiormente quedando en la Capital el Governador con la Tropa indicada al parrafo 61. y no existir yà la feroz Nacion de los Tobosos, que eran los que antes insultaban las Provincias.

88. Movido de iguales razones huviera propuesto tambien la extincion de el Presidio de la Mesa del Tonati titulado Sn Franco Xavier en la Provincia del Nayarit, por que estando en situacion tan distante, y à trasmano de las Provincias insultadas, de nada avia podido servirles su fuerza, ni darles auxilio; y solamente dixe, no poder asegurar si conducia el que subsistiesse al primer fin de su ereccion.

89. Manifesté si, que se hallaba en el centro de la

Sierra, y en el de muchos Pueblos de Españoles, y
de Indios, y Missiones: que sabia averse sublevado
sus individuos varias veces, intentando la expulsion de sus Ministros, y que desde el año de 54, h.ta
el de 63. avian mantenido la Guerra contra el Presidio, y Fronteras de la Costa de el Sur, poniendo en
precision al Govierno de dictar providencias oportunas à su castigo, y concluio con que por no tener instruccion bastante para opinar con certeza, tampoco
podia dar dictamen seguro sobre si convenia, ò nò
su extincion.

90. No sucedio assi por lo respectivo al Presidio de
S.n Antonio de Bexar, pues aviendoseme pedido
parecer en el asunto, expuse desde luego debia quedar en èl la compañia de su dotacion, que se compone de quarenta y un hombres inclusos el Capitan, y el Capellan, y agregada à ella la de S.n
Agustin de Ahumada en el Orcoquisac, que la
servia de refuerzo por disposicion de el Govierno
precedente al actual, y constaba de un Capitan con
treinta, y una Plazas.

91. Este refuerzo me parecio bastante para resguardo de aquel terreno, teniendo consideracion à
que la corta diferencia de diez hombres, se suplia
ventajosamente con los vecinos de la Villa de San
Fernando que debian salir à campaña en las urgen-
cias, y con mas de cincuenta Indios, que supe apron-
taron graciosamente para tales casos los Padres Ministros de las cinco Missiones immediatas, muni-

cionados, y bastimentados de Cavallos, Armas, y demas preciso.

92. Seguiasse de tal determinacion el ahorro à la R.l Hacienda de tres mil, y ochocientos pesos cada año, por importar la baxa delas diez Plazas esta cantidad al respecto de trescientos ochenta pesos cada una, à mas de que podia salir un Capitan con la Tropa conveniente, ò àperseguir los Barbaros del Norte, si continuaban sus hostilidades, ò à facilitar la reduccion delos infieles à la costa.

93. Ocupabame, pues, en el desempeño de estos, y otros asuntos de mi cargo, quando entre muchas dudosas noticias que tenia dela oposicion de los Capitanes de Presidios al importante acertado proyecto dela linea en los parages determinados, recibi la cierta de que el Governador de Coahuila se oponia abiertamente à la translacion de Presidios à las margenes del Rio grande se el Norte, que la R.l Junta tenia aprobado: pero aviendo Yo representado en Carta de 21. de Julio de 72. lo que me parecio proprio demi zelo en obsequio del servicio, quedó ilusorio quanto se avia expuesto en contra, pues la misma Real Junta que comprendio, acaso, los resortes de q.e tal Oposicion dimanaba en este Gefe, y en los demas Capitanes de Presidios, resolvio que nada se innovasse.

94. Entre tanto que tales disenciones se cuestionaban, fueron succesivamente arribando à

Chiguagua las Cavalladas mandadas comprar, y el respectivo armamento para las quatro Compañías volantes de la Expedicion, à quienes se repartio todo, desde luego, para poder empezar Yo mis operaciones.

95. Yà con tal auxilio acordé estas con los Governadores de las Provincias de Sonora, Vizcaya, y Coahuila, y determiné mi salida à reconocer el confluente del Rio grande del Norte, à que se resultas se trasladaron los Presidios de Cerro gordo, Julimes, Monclova, Sta Rosa, y Sn Saba, haciendo depaso el desalojo de los muchos Yndios que se hallaban arranchados en el Bolson de Mapimi, con la precision de que se pasassen al opuesto lado de aquel Rio: cosa que hicieron gustosos, ò forzados por el castigo que sobre sí imaginaban, y en efecto podian temerle, por que nunca tube esperanzas mas completas de conseguirlo, segun la calidad de mis dispociciones.

96. Entre tanto se hallaba puesta à cubierto en lo posible la Provincia de Nueva Vizcaya, pues à mas de las partidas destinadas al resguardo de Chiguagua, y su circunferencia, avia otras que cortaban el terreno, y todas baxo el mando del Theniente Coronel dn Manuel Muñoz, cuis espiritu militar, animosidad, y practico conocimiento, me precisaron à confiarselo; y para la mas completa seguridad de los terrenos del Oriente de aquella Villa, dispuse que una partida

de veinte hombres à cargo de un Oficial de el Presidio de Guaxuquilla, se apostasse en el sitio nombrado el Ancòn de Carros, y providencié que otra de igual numero se mantubiesse en las immediaciones del Pueblo de S.ⁿ Jeronimo, sin otra que debia cortar las entradas de el parage llamado la Noria, y Cañada del Fresno, sitios todos por donde los Indios estaban acostumbrados à hacer sus mas frecuentes incursiones.

97.   Dictadas estas providencias, salì à la indicada Expedicion acompañado delas primera, tersera, y quarta Compañias Volantes, y despues de prolixas, y penosas maniobras, no solo consegui el desalojo referido, sino hacer veer à los Barbaros lo que eran las Armas de el Rey, quando se trataba formalmente de hacerlas gloriosas, aunque por mano tan inferior como la mia, si bien las providencias de el Altissimo de qualquiera instrumento se valen.

98.   Por este tiempo llegò à mis manos el nuevo Rolamento de Presidios con la instruccion formada por el Govierno, y con arreglo à una, y à otra, demarquè por depronto el terreno que debian ocupar los Presidios de Monclova, y Santa Rosa, previo el correspondiente examen; y dexando sus respectivas Compañias en los trabajos de sus nuevas fabricas, con el auxilio conducente à no impedir sus progressos, continuè mi marcha por todo el citado Rio, señalando los

sitios que actualmente ocupan en la linea los Presidios de S.ⁿ Antonio Bucareli, S.ⁿ Sabá, San Carlos, y el dela Junta delos Rios, y me regresé à Chiguagua, sin mas resulta en varios choques que tube con los Barbaros que la perdida de un soldado que murio de sus heridas.

99.   A los ocho dias demi arribo à Chiguagua, fue forzoso pasasse à la Revista de Inspeccion, y arreglasse las Compañias que guarnesen los tres Presidios nominados entonces cerro gordo, Guaxuquilla, y Julimes: y aviendo practicado en los meses de Julio, y Agosto de el expresado año de 73. con la prolijidad que acreditan lo documentos dirigidos à este Superior Govierno, me regressé à la Villa, à fin de proveerme delos Viveres necesarios para las subsecuentes operaciones.

100.   Hechas las prevenciones correspondientes, y para que no se verificasse la introduccion de enemigos à lo interior dela Provincia, dispuse guarnecer con Escuadras dela tercera, y quarta Compañias Volantes dela Expedicion toda la Frontera desde la Sierra de Carretas hasta el ojo caliente, y que la primera Compañia entrasse por el rumbo de el Sur à reconocer el Bolson de Mapimi, debiendose encontrar conmigo en el Rio grande de el Norte, y parage llamado S.ⁿ Carlos: destiné la segunda para el resguardo dela Villa de Chiguagua, y sus contornos con las ordenes, è instrucciones delo que debian observar en sus respectivos terrenos los

Oficiales que se nombraron para el mando de las Escuadras que debian resguardar la Frontera. Salí de Chiguagua à principios de el mes de Octubre de 73. con las dos Compañias de Dragones de España, y Mexico que yà hacian el servicio en ella: y dirigiendo mi marcha al Presidio de Tulimes, dispuse que en él se incorporassen conmigo los removentes de el Cerro gordo, y Guaxuquilla con sus familias, y demas necesarios à su establecimiento en el Rio grande de el Norte.

101. Continué mi marcha con todo este embarazoso tren hasta el citado Rio, y dexando à cada uno de estos Presidios en sus respectivos terrenos, me regressé con las dos Compañias de Dragones al de la Junta de los Rios Norte, y Conchos: y al segundo dia de mi arrivo, divisó la Centinela una polvadera que venia por todo el Rio, y era, como discurri, la compañia de Dn Domingo Diaz que debia incorporarseme, cuio ofical me informó que en todo el Bolson de Mapimi no se hallaba una pisada de Yndios, desde el ultimo reconocimiento que Jo hice de aquellos terrenos.

102. Evacuadas las antecedentes maniobras con felicidad; y deseando encontrar modo para que los nuevos Presidios pudiessen trabaxar en las fabricas materiales de sus recintos sin ser molestados de los enemigos, discurri que el mas seguro à conseguirlo, seria el castigo de estos en sus mismas Rancherias. Salí en efecto con tal

destino áel Presidio ála Junta álos Ríos, y cruzando
el grande áel Norte à principios áe Noviembre del
año áe 73. asistido áe las dos Compañias áe Dragones,
y la primera ála expedicion seguí mi marcha p.ᵃ
el Rio Colorado con las precauciones debidas hasta
el dia 26. áe dicho mes que me avisaron las Escuadras que cortaban por derecha, è izquierda aver
hallado una huella crecida, que se introducia à la
espesa Sierra áel Mogano.

103.   Por ser entonces áe noche dispuse acampar mi
Tropa en el Ojo áe agua que se halla à la falda áe
la Sierra à fin de descansar áe las fatigas que
avia sufrido en las rapidas marchas que era
forzoso hacer, particularmente en los dos ultimos
dias que andubimos sin parar de dia, ni de noche
para alcanzar à los Indios, que suponiamos hui-
an áe nosotros. Aprovecheme áela Luna que
hacia, y con doce hombres salí à reconocer la
Sierra, cuia aspereza no dió lugar à que pudiesse
demarcar el terreno, ò parte áela que ocupaban
los enemigos, bien que estos, y por medio áelas señas
que hacian sus espias, nos daban á entender que
allí estaban. Como à media noche me regressè
al Campo, y disponiendo todo lo necesario para
atacarlos à la madrugada áe el dia siguiente 27.
áe Noviembre marchè con mi Tropa para la Sierra, è internandome por uno áe sus Caxones,
y sobre la huella áelos enemigos en distancia
áe una legua, y en lo mas aspero áella me

49

[49]

atacaron con mucho brio, y valor mas de seis-
cientos Indios, pero la Alta Providencia de
quien todo pende me concedio sobre ellos la
mas completa Victoria, sin que de nuestra parte
huviera avido mas averia que la de dos Salda-
dos que salieron levemente heridos, à cuia
gloriosa funcion constantemente debe atribuir-
se la conclusion delas fabricas delos Presidios
de el Oriente, pues desde ella no se dexaron veer
los enemigos en mucho tiempo.

104.   Despues de esta Campaña me retirè al Presidio delas Juntas el dia 30. de Diciembre, de
donde sali el dia 3. al reconocimiento, arreglo, y
translacion delos Presidios de el Poniente, por lo
mucho que urgia su cumplimiento: y siguiendo
mi marcha con cincuenta hombres bastante.m.te
expuesto por su corto numero, y los rigorosos
frios de los meses de el Invierno, consegui à ex-
pensas de infinitas fatigas demarcar el terreno
en que avian de ubicarse los Presidios de el
Principe, S.n Eleseario, S.n Fernando del Carrizal, S.n Buenaventura, y Janos: y pasando Rvis-
ta à sus respectivas Compañias los traslade à
los terrenos en que oy existen.

105.   Vuelto à Chiguagua tube orden del Govierno para transferirme à la Provincia de Coahuila. Verifique esto el dia 27 de Marzo de 1774. despues de dictadas las disposiciones que regulè proprias al resguardo, è hize lo proprio en Coahuila

50

encargando su cumplimiento al Governador Dn.
Jacobo de Ugarte, y Loyola.

106. Este viage me proporcionó ocasion de recorrer
de nuevo la linea, y de reconocer el estado de las
fabricas materiales de los Presidios, como el en que
se hallaban sus respectivas Compañias, en cuia
importante ocupacion me mantube hasta fin de
Noviembre del proprio año, en que dispuse una
salida con el oboeto de castigar à los Barbaros, que
supe hallarse arranchados en unas Sierras distan-
tes sesenta leguas de el Presidio de Janos, rumbo
al Norueste, desde donde salian à incomodar la
Frontera con sus rapiñas.

107. Venturosamente conseguido el castigo, y apre-
hension de ellos, mandè conducirlos al Presidio del
Carrizal, para precaver assí todo riesgo, y el dia
15. de Enero me transferi al Paso del Norte con
destino à formar las Compañias de Milicias preveni-
das en la Ordenanza: en cuio Pueblo hallará V.S.
por resultas de esta operacion quatro, cada una de
cincuenta, y tres hombres inclusos los Oficiales.

108. Hecha esta diligencia volvi al Presidio de el
Carrizal, donde hè solido recidir las cortas tempo-
radas que me lo hàn permitido las atenciones
de el mando: alli formalizè el plan de operaciones
para la campaña general que tenia premeditada,
y dirigido al Govierno merecio su aprobacion, y
yo me dispuse à practicarla.

109. Con este intento sali de el Carrizal para

Chiguagua el dia 30. de Marzo. Di las ordenes oportunas al acopio de viveres. Me desembararé de la porcion de piezas apresadas en mis salidas, remitiendolas à esta Capital à cargo de el Capitan de Dragones d.n Manuel Pardo. Formé el Reglamento por que se goviernan las quatro Companias Volantes con aprovacion de esta superioridad: y resuelto à pasar à Sonora para volver à tiempo de hacer la Campaña, me trasladé à aquella Provincia el 22. de Mayo: en ella revisté, y arreglé las Compañias Presidiales; reconoci los terrenos en que debian ubicarse los quatro Presidios de Fronteras, Terrenate, Tubac, y S.ta Gertrudis del Altar; hice el informe general de mis observaciones en aquella Provincia, y previa la aprobacion de el Govierno, determiné la translacion de el primero al Valle de S.n Bernardino; la de el segundo al Sitio nombrado S.ta Cruz; la de el tercero al de S.n Agustin de el Tuquison; y la de el quarto al de Escomac, regresandome despues à la Frontera de Nueva Vizcaya, para prevenir lo conducente à la indicada Campaña General.

110.   En 13. de Septiembre arribé sin novedad al Presidio de S.n Buenaventura, y sin mas descanso que el de seis dias, verifiqué mi nueva salida consiguiendo afortunadamente el fin q.e me avia propuesto de castigar, y escarmentar à los Barbaros, entre cuias resultas fue feliz la reduccion de los Apaches Navajoes à sus antiguos

Pueblos, de quienes estaban hostilizadas las dos Provincias de Vizcaya, y Nuevo Mexico.

111.   Por los adjuntos Estados Numeros 1º 2º y 3º reconocerá V.S. el numero de Presidios con distincion de Provincias de que se compone la nueva linea formada de Mar à Mar; la entera conclusion de sus fabricas materiales excepto algunas obras interiores que faltan à los de Monclava, y Santa Rosa, y las de los tres de la Provincia de Sonora Sta Cruz, Sn Agustin del Tuquison, y Sta Gertrudis del Altar, bien que estas es probable se concluian en corto tiempo, segun el auxilio de Indios que les franquean las dos Misiones de San Xavier del Vac, y Sn Agustin, y no se han movido de sus antiguos terrenos los dos de la Bahia del Espiritu Santo, y Sn Juan Baptista del Rio Grande, por estar ambos en linea, y prevenido assi en la Rl Instruccion.

112.   En dichos Documentos verá V.S. tambien la fuerza efectiva de los Presidios; la del Cuerpo Volante de la Expedicion, y Milicias de el Pueblo del Paso; el situado de Cavallada, y Mulada, y el costo anual que tiene al Rey toda linea con expresion de Sueldos, en que se incluie el de el Inspector de Presidios, y sus dos Ayudantes.

113.   Toda la Tropa Presidial es de calidad superior en Talla, y robustez de valor, y constancia para la fatiga de su penoso instituto, mui diestra en manejarse à Cavallo, y en las evoluciones utiles, y adaptables

53

à la especie de Guerra que hacen. En las muchas
funciones de que hè sido testigo han acreditado instruccion en el manejo delas Armas, amor al servicio, y afanoso deseo de castigar à los Barbaros,
para lo qual no han perdonado riesgos ni fatigas, antes por el contrario han sufrido gustosos hambre, sed,
y las demas incomodidades que produce continuam.te
la guerra, quando se hace en Paises tan dilatados,
y despoblados, como los que và à mandar V.S.

114.   Cada Soldado tenia existentes quando dexé
el mando los siete Cavallos, y una Mula que les
señala la Ordenanza. El vestuario de que usa aquella Tropa es uniforme en todas las Provincias, y consta de una Chupa corta de Tripe, ò paño azul con
una pequeña buelta, y Collarin encarnado, boton
dorado, Calzon de Tripe azul, capa de paño de el
mismo color, Cartuchera, Cuera, y Vandoleras de
Gamuza, en la que se halla bordado el nombre del
Presidio, Corbatin negro, Sombrero, Zapatos, y Botines: y todo se hallaba en buen uso, quando Yo
me separè delas Fronteras.

115.   El Armamento constaba de espada ancha
de el tamaño, y hechura que usa la demas Cavalleria de el Exercito, Lanza, Adarga, Escopeta, y
Pistolas. De el que de orden de el Rey se hà remi-
tido à aquellas Fronteras para el uso de sus Presidios, se hallaba el repuesto correspondiente, y descon-
tado su total importe à favor dela R.l Hacienda por
los Oficiales Reales de San Luis, Potosi, Real delos

llamos, y el Thesorero de la Villa de Chiguagua.

116.	En el Almacen de cada uno delos Presidios se hallaba existente el repuesto de Polvora correspondiente à ocho libras por Plaza arreglada, y al resguardo de dos llaves delas quales tenia el Capitan una, y otra el Oficial habilitado.

117.	La Montura se reducia à una Silla Baquera, con las cubiertas correspondientes llamadas Mochila, Coraza, Armas, Coginillos, y Estribos de palo: y todo estaba de buen uso al tiempo de mi separacion.

118.	En las Caxas de gratificacion de diez pesos por Plaza se hallaron existentes las correspondientes al tiempo desde que hè puesto las Compañias sobre el nuevo pie de Ordenanza, hasta fin de Diciembre del año proximo anterior (à excepcion dela delos Presidios de Monclava, Sta Rosa, y el de el Principe, cuios Capitanes no han observado los articulos dela Rl. Instruccion) y leyales las cuentas presentadas delos gastos comunes que se han ofrecido, cuios documentos se depositaron en las mismas para su constancia: y para el caido que de cien pesos por Plaza debe tener cada Soldado en Caxa para los fines que expresa el Articulo 2º Tit.º 5º dela Rl. Instruccion, se han hecho las retenciones de veinte pesos anuales à cada uno, cuio fondo se hallaba depositado en Caxas de tres llaves, y de estas una en poder de cada uno de los Oficiales dela Compañia.

119.	Con la formacion dela linea de Presidios, queda abierta la libre comunicacion delas Provincias de

Texas, Coahuila, Vizcaya, Sonora, y Nueva Mex.
y en cada Presidio establecido el methodo que deben
observar para el servicio diario, y cosadas que continuamente hande practicar sus Esquadras; el en q.e
deben formalizar los ajustamientos de Caxa, estados de debitos, y creditos de cada Compañia; mem-
bretes para la liquidacion de la cuenta particular
de el Soldado, y la general de el Oficial habilitado,
para estender las filiaciones de las Reclutas que
en adelante se hicieren para las revistas, y diarios
que de sus operaciones deben remitir mensalm.te;
Lisas de la fuerza efectiva de sus respectivas Compañias; estados de Vestuario, Armamento, y Mon-
tura; Rejimen que hande guardar para el despacho de los Correos mensuales, con los demas documentos, è instrucciones que libré, y conducen al
mas acertado, puro govierno de las Compañias
Presidiales; forma en que estas han de hacer sus
campañas, y una noticia instructiva de las Sierras, Cañadas, Aguages, y Terrenos que comun.te
habitan los Enemigos, de cuio conocimiento care-
cian hasta ahora en general las Tropas Presidiales.

120.   Todos estos progressos se han verificado à
costa de mucha vigilancia, y de un infatigable
zelo por el servicio, sin el acaso se hallaria la
Frontera mas invadida, y nadie como Yo hà conocido lo que vale la presencia de el Jefe en todas partes. En quantas funciones tube con los

[56]

Barbaros salí dichosamente victorioso, Restableciendo el honor de las Armas del Rey, que se hallaba decadente quando tomè el mando de aquellas Provincias.

121.	Para conseguirlo no hè perdonado tiempo, fatiga, ni incomodidad; y si V.S. para la consideracion en que en el corto tiempo de poco mas de cinco años hè peregrinado por parages ignorados, por Sierras y Cañadas incognitas, y por Montes, y Rios desconocidos, andando al pie de quatro mil leguas, en q. por mi proprio hè transmigrado los Presidios de Sonora, y Vizcaya; revistado, y arreglado sus Compañias, y desalojado à los Enemigos de los vastos terrenos que ocupaban en distancia de setecientas leguas de Oriente à Poniente, y doscientas de Norte à Sur, conocerà la diferencia que ai de el estado de la Frontera comparado con el que tenia el año de 74. Entonces estaban los Barbaros llenos de insolencia, y orgullo por las ventajas que à cada paso conseguian, y un corto numero de ellos se atrevia à duplicada fuerza nuestra, como lo testifican varios exemplares; oy sucede todo al contrario, y siempre que se continuen las cortadas que dispuse, y en la Oficialidad halla la constancia, y valor à que se iban acostumbrando, y no se dexen sorprender, como alguna vez se hà visto, vivirán los Barbaros contenidos, segun lo que quedan de escarmentados.

122.	Muchas funciones pudiera referir para comprobar esta asercion, pero, pues, V.S. tiene en el

Archivo de Chiguagua documentos bien corroboran
tes de ellas, bastará que Yo apunte la que el animo
so, y experimentado Oficial d.n Narciso Tapia tu
bo con los esforzados Yndios del Poniente en el
parage dla Estancia de Becerra que tanta glo
ria dió à las Armas del Monarca, y la que
mandé Yo por mi persona en el caxon del Mo
gano, de que resultó el nuevo Cordon de Presidios,
que dificultosamente se huviera verificado à no
averse los Barbaros preocupado de terror por
el descalabro que recibieron.

123.　　Aunque por el nuevo Reglamento se man
dan extinguir los dos Presidios de S.n Miguel
de Orcasitas, y S.n Carlos de Buenavista en Sono
ra, no quiso el Govierno hacer novedad hasta que
Yo pasasse à la Provincia, y revistasse los remo
ventes. Antes de este caso se avia consultado la
translacion de aquellos dos à las margenes de los
Rios Colorado, y Gila, y Yo opiné lo mismo, bien
que dexando alguna fuerza en los dos sitios que
ocupan, para lo qual, y hasta la radicación de
los Yndios Seris, y Suaquis, pedi se subrrogasse
en su lugar la Compañia Volante.

124.　　Transmigrandose còmo el Rey tiene apro
bado los dos referidas Presidios à los Rios indi
cados, es verosimil la consecucion de faborables
progresos entre las muchas Naciones que hà ex
plorado ultimamente el Padre Misionero Fr.
Francisco Garcez entre la Provincia del Moqui,

y nuevas adquisiciones de la California, ŏ por lo menos se mantendrà libre el camino de ellas, que hà abierto el Theniente Coronel d.ⁿ Juan Baptista de Anza, siempre que las Naciones Yumas, y demas que acaban de declararse amigas persistan firmes en su intencion.

125.   En el Archivo de Chiguagua hallarà V.S. originales las disposiciones sobre el modo de hacer los pagamentos dela Tropa, ministrarles Polvora, y por que mano, como tambien la dictada con relacion al reintegro de el importe de Armamento que debe repartirse à los Soldados quando lo necesiten.

126.   Casi todos los Presidios se hallan con el repuesto de Armas que la Real Ordenanza previene; pero no sucediendo assi con el Cuerpo Volante de la Expedicion, de quien pende el principal resguardo de las Fronteras, convendrà que para que esta Tropa no carezca de este auxilio tan indispensable à sus operaciones succesivas, se les provea de las necesarias con arreglo à su fuerza efectiva.

127.   Las reglas que por su constitucion observan las Tropas Presidiales son guardar su Presidio, y Cavallada; dar para acopio, y conduccion de viveres, y efectos que sus guarniciones necesitan la Escolta suficiente; correr los Terrenos immediatos; auxiliarse reciprocamente las partidas destacadas à ello; y hacer segun las Ordenes del Jefe las Campañas que se dispongan.

59

128.　　Las de el Cuerpo Volante, se emplean tambien en los acopios, y transportes de viveres, y efectos que demanda su subsistencia, manteniendose continuamente sus Escuadras en cortar todo el basto terreno, que intermedia desde la Sierra de Caretas que està al Poniente de el Presidio de Tanos, hasta el de Sn. Antonio Bucareli primero de Coahuila, y desde el Parage llamado Ancon de Camos hasta el Presidio viejo de el Gallo, y circunferencia de Chiguagua, sin que por esto deven de hacer sus Campañas respectivas.

129.　　Sin embargo de estas disposiciones que mi conocimiento, y experiencias me han hecho creer oportunas, es imposible impedir de el todo las rapiñas, y robos que los Barbaros executan en lo interior de la Provincia, pero por lo regular suelen ser Cuadrillas pequeñas que logran introducirse sin ser vistas por el mismo Cordon de Presidios.

130.　　Assi se hà verificado en mi tiempo, y podrà experimentarse en lo successivo, si se atiende à la sutileza con que algunos Indios Peloteros suelen introducirse. Con todo siempre que se cotejen las incursiones, y daños de estos ultimos tiempos, con las que los Barbaros cometian antes de la formacion de el Cuerpo Volante, y establecerse la nueva planta, se veran de bulto las ventajas conseguidas; pues à mas de que no hàn sido tan repetidas las muertes, y robos, no se han experimentado los despuebles de Lugares, Haciendas, ni Ranchos algunos que cada dia se notaban; antes por el contrario se vèn repoblados desde entonce acà, como consta de Autos, muchos que avian quedado Yermos: y sobre todo la propria Villa de Chiguagua es un testigo de excepcion que podrà deponer sobre la tranquilidad q. goza con restitucion de masde siete mil Bestias hecha en mi tiempo, de las que à los Indios han podido quitarse. Sentado lo qual, y que tales felices efectos corresponden directamente al bien dela Frontera en general, paso à decir los que corresponden à la Tropa en particular, y las consecuencias que de ello se siguen al servicio.

Efectos provechosos que hà producido la nueva Planta.

131. Segun la antigua Planta de Presidios, y à proporcion delas distancias en que se hallaban de esta Corte, gozaban sus individuos distintos Sueldos: unos quatrocientos y veinte pesos: otros quatrocientos, y algunos trescientos, y ochenta, cuias aberes se les subministraban por los respectivos Capitanes en Generos, sin que halla exemplar de averse dado un peso en reales, por cuia falta, y circulacion hà resultado no huviesse Poblaciones, ni Comercio de consideracion en las Fronteras, pues es constante que los Capitanes con

motivo de engrosar sus Caudales impedian con
graves penas la entrada à sus Presidios delos Co-
merciantes, y demas Gente que creian pudiessen
perjudicarles.

132.   Al Soldado que en aquellos tiempos mas
sueldo gozaba, no tocaban cien pesos cabales al
año, segun las cuentas del libro de Caxa, que
assi el Señor Marqués de Rubi, como Jo, liqui-
damos varias veces.

133.   De tan dolosa practica se seguia el empeño
de quatrocientos, y mas pesos en el Soldado àl
fin de el año, de que resultaba la inaccion de
este, aun en el caso de invasion de Enemigos,
como muchas veces hà sucedido, pues recelando
el Capitan que con la muerte de el Soldado per-
deria sin duda el empeño de este, nunca per-
mitia saliesse la Tropa de el Presidio à contener
los enemigos en sus hostilidades, pero aun co-
incidieron otras muchas consideraciones de abu-
sos, y excessos que se tubieron presentes p.a
la formacion de el Real Reglamento de diez
de Septiembre de 1772.

134.   Por el feliz establecimiento de este se hà lo-
grado redimir à la Tropa de sus antiguas ve-
jaciones, pues aunque por la misma no goza
el Soldado masque doscientos, y noventa pesos
de sueldo al año, y diez de gratificacion, logra
la grandissima ventaja de recibir por mano del
Oficial habilitado los efectos al costo, y costas,

como assi mismo dos reales diarios que en especie
sele subministra àpresencia de toda la Compañia; y finalmente seles entrega el alcance, que
algunos suelen hacer de treinta, quarenta, sesenta,
ochenta, y hasta de cien pesos al habilitado à fin
de año; siendo mas apreciable que todo la livertad q.
disputan de poder comprar sus efectos en donde
mas cuenta les tenga.

135.   De esta piadosa providencia no solo se deduce
la equidad con que debe ser tratado el Soldado,
sino que tambien con la circulacion del dinero
efectivo en aquellas Provincias, se logra la concu-
rrencia de muchas gentes, quedando algunas radi-
cadas en ellas, y aquel en aptitud de hacer el
servicio, exponiendo gloriosamente su vida, si_
empre que se ofrece ocasion, como se hà veri_
ficado repetidas veces, sin que al Capitan quede
el recelo de que con su muerte pueda perder al_
gunos intereses.

136.   Conocida, pues, la utilidad de quantos puntos
contiene la R.ᵉ Ynstruccion, debe en mi concepto
observarse puntualmente su cumplimiento, no
permitiendo jamas que en tan importante
asunto haya variacion alguna por las fata_
lissimas consecuencias que podia producir qua_
lesquiera innovacion que se hiciera.

137.   Acaso avrà quien proponga con cedori_
dos la utilidad de establecer en la Frontera
una, dos, ò tres Factorias, suponiendo lo con_

veniente que será proveerse en ella los Habilitados de los avios necesarios para la subsistencia de sus respectivos Presidios; y si se practicase
assi seria destruir enteramente las piadosas, sa-
bias, y utiles reglas que prescribe la R.l Instruccion para el manejo de caudales.

138.   Si la desgracia de las Provincias internas
llegare à tanta, como esta, estancando por consi-
quiente entre una, dos, ò tres personas algo mas
de medio millon de pesos, que anualmente circu-
la entre sus individuos, se verà entonces, y con
dolor, no solo el disgusto general de la Tropa, sino
tambien el total despueble de aquellos Paises, y
repetidas quexas de el Comercio, como à quien mas
directamente se perjudica.

139.   Para evitar tan funestas resultas, no ai medio
mas seguro, que el que proporciona la R.l Instruccion, haciendo observar el cumplimiento de ella
en todas sus partes, y con la exactitud que en
mi tiempo se hà verificado, pues de no hacerlo
assi, serà, segun alcanzo, cortar los progressos
à que se dirige, y arruinar las Provincias en
vez de hacerlas opulentas, como el Rey desea, y
conviene à la felicidad de su corona.

Calidad de Indios q.̃ hostilizan la Frontera.

140.   Los Apaches que consternan las Provincias
de Sonora, y Nueva Vizcaya son conocidos

por los nombres Chiricagui, Gileños, Mimbrere-
ños, Mescaleros, Faraones, Rancherias de Pascual, y el Lisero, la de Alonso, la de el Capitan
Vigotes, y el Natagé. Los tres primeros en len-
gua Apache se llaman Sigilande, Seroende,
Chiguende, y las restantes Zetroende, Selcotisanende, Culcahende, Cachuginde, Yncagende, Sigilande, y Zetroende.

141.   Las tres primeras Naciones espresadas re-
siden comunmente en las dilatadas, y asperas Si-
erras de Chiricagui, Gila, Mimbres, la Florida,
Cerro gordo, Sangre de Christo, Corral de San
Agustin, Capulin, Corral de Piedra, la Sierra
obcura, la Blanca, la de el Sacramento, los
Organos, Peraca, Sierra de los Ladrones, la de la
Magdalena, la de Enmedio, el Ojo de Abeitia,
Sierra de la Hacha, las Espuelas, la Mogina, la
Boca, Corral de Quintero, Mesas de Robledo
Sierras de el Paso de el Norte, Cerro hueco, S.n
Nicolas, y otras varias que se hallan en frente
de los Presidios de Sonora, y los tres de el Ponien-
te de la Viscaya, Janos, S.n Buenaventura,
y S.n Fernando de el Carrizal, y las restan-
tes Naciones abrazan todo el Terreno, que se
halla al lado opuesto de el Rio grande de el
Norte hasta el Colorado abrigandose de las sierras
que corren de Poniente al Oriente, llamadas la de
Guadalupe, Mogano, Sierra Nevada, Chanate, la del
Cornudo, la de el Ayre, cola de el Aguila, Sierra

del Diablo, y su Cordillera hasta el Rio de S.n Pedro, de donde comunmente salen estos Yndios à come- ter sus hostilidades, assi en la Provincia de Nue- va Vizcaya, como en la de Coahuila, de modo q.e solo el Natagé es poco afecto à las Sierras, por cuio motivo se arrancha lo mas de el tiempo en las orillas de el Rio Colorado, y parages llamados los Arenales, y Poros.

Guerra que acostumbran hacer.

142.   Estos Barbaros habitan segun las estaciones de el año aquellos parages que les ofrece la mejor proporcion para su manutencion, y pastos para sus Cavalladas, pero siempre en lo interior, mas oculto, y resguardado de las Sierras, consultando à la seguridad de sus mugeres, è hijos, y de sus siembras de Maises, y otros fructos, pero sin la precision de mantener, y conservar estos terre- nos, por tener en qualquiera otro lo mismo.

143.   Los hombres de Armas andan ordinariam.te fuera de sus Rancherias, y casi incesantemente sobre nuestro terreno, sin otro destino que el de robar, y hacer todos los daños que pueden.

144.   El vestido de los hombres se compone de un Patigo, y unos Cueros de Gamusa, ò de Cybolo, su comida la que les ofrece el Campo librada en sus Armas, comiendo toda especie de Animales en particular los Cavallos, y Mulas, y varias Yerbas,

y raices.

145.   Sus Armas son el churo, õ lanza, y el Arco, y Flechas: sus chimales, que entre nosotros es la Adarga, õ Broquel, y algunas Cueras. Tienen porcion de Armas de fuego, que adquirieron en cambalache delos Indios Vidais que residen inmediatos à la Lusitania; y Cavallos con abundancia, assi por los muchos que han robado, como por los que crian, pues les sirve de alimenta.

146.   Andan siempre Volantes en diversas Escuadras sobre nuestros Terrenos, y Caminos. Ellos como practicos de la tierra ocupan los Puestos que les son mas ventajosos: previenen igualm.te los asaltos, pero de suerte que nunca se hà verificado, ni verificarà el que se presente à los nuestros igual numero de ellos, sino siempre con tan conocido excesso, que es como cierta su Victoria, y como no esten precisados à defenderse, resguardar, ni mantener parage, sitio, ni Poblacion alguna, esperan, quando es incomparablem.te maior su numero; y huien, quando se consideran pocos.

147.   De todo lo qual se infiere ser este un genero de Enemigos, que para continuar la Guerra por muchos años no necesitan delas providencias que toda gente politica, como son caudales, Subsidios para pagamentos, Armas, Municiones, Viveres, y Bastimentos; Muladas para las conducciones, y acarreos; Recultas de Gente; acopios

de Granos, y otras muchas prevenciones indispensables para el efecto, pues todos son Soldados vete-
ranos, y aun Criados en la Guerra, pagados, mu-
nicionados, y bastimentados en qualquiera parage, tiempo, y ocasion; sin otro empleo, ocupacion,
ni oficio necesario para su manutencion, ni la de
sus mugeres, è hijos.

148. En el año pasado de 1773. y con total arreglo à
las prudentes advertencias de este Superior Govierno,
se hicieron las paces con los Indios Lipanes, y estos
segun entiendo se han mantenido desde entonces
acà sosegados, à exepcion de algunos que de ellos
suelen juntarse con los Mezcaleros à cometer
sus robos, y muertes.

149. Como quiera que la Nacion entera de estos
Indios Lipanes hà procurado mantenerse constante en la fee prometida, no parece regular que
por los excessos cometidos por algunos de sus individuos, se solicite el castigo de toda ella, el que
en tal caso no admite pocas dificultades, y à la
verdad puede producir amarguissimas consecuencias.

150. Esto asentado, soi de parecer, que estos Indios
deben ser tratados del mismo modo que el Rey
manda en el Art. 6. Tit. 10. de la R.l Instruccion
de 10. de Septiembre de 72: y de que seles conser-
ve el mejor trato, y correspondencia disimulan-
doles algunas faltas, ò leves excessos, y procurando inducirlos con el buen exemplo, y persuasion

àque admitan Misioneros, y se reduzcan à la dominacion de el Rey.

151.   Si alguna vez hicieren (como suelen) robo de Cavallada, ù otro exceso que no conviene disimular, y requeridos no lo restituiessen, seles puede obligar con la fuerza, haciendoles el menos daño q.e sea posible, à fin de no exasperar los animos dela Nacion entera, por las esperanzas que ai de que se podrà con el tiempo, y trato con los Españoles lograr su apetecida reduccion à Misiones, ô Pueblos.

152.   Dexando para despues tratar dela Provincia de Fexas que se halla mas de un grado fuera de nuestra linea, y las bastas belicosas Naciones del Norte que la circundan pasarè à dar una idea dela guerra defensiva, y ofensiva, que segun conceptuo debe hacerse à los Apaches, que hostilizan las Provincias de Sonora, Nueva Vizcaya, Nuevo Mexico, y Coahuila, assi para impedir las rapiñas de dichos Enemigos, como para sugetarlos à la Real Dominacion.

153.   Para el logro de tan importante obgeto se halla en las Fronteras un Cordon de Presidios, que abraza quinientas leguas poco mas, ô menos desde el Presidio dela Bahia del Espiritu Santo hasta el de S.ta Gertrudis del Altar: El cuerpo Volante de la Expedicion; y dos Piquetes de Dragones, que de Real ôrñ hacen el servicio en ellas.

154.   Teniendo, pues, la Guerra defensiva por obgeto el impedir la entrada delos Enemigos à lo interior

delas Provincias; seguir, y castigar à los que con
sutileza pueden introducirse por nuestro Presidio,
facilitando por este medio el sosiego de los moradores de aquellos Paises, giro de sus Comercios, libertad delos caminos Rs, y seguridad delos bienes
de Campo; el medio mas seguro para conseguirlo
será siempre la vigilancia delas Escuadras, que se
destinen en sus respectivos Terrenos, à cubrir, y
correr diariamente la Campaña en los Lugares
que intermedian de un Presidio à otro en la forma que hasta aqui se há practicado, socorrien-
dose mutuamente; pues por el Derrotero que
à cada una se asigna, les será facil saber el
parage, ò parages en que pueden hallarse, y por
si mis reglas fueren adaptables, describiré à V.S. las
que discurro para la maior seguridad de las
Fronteras.

155.   Las Escuadras delos Presidios, y el Cuerpo Volante
dela expedicion, deberan componerse del numero
de hombres, y Oficiales que el Comandante en Jefe,
tubiere por conveniente señalar à cada uno, y
con atencion al delos enemigos.

Presidio de Sta Gertrudis del Altar.

156.   La Escuadra de este Presidio deberá correr hasta la Mision despoblada de Sonoitac, y desde
alli hasta el nuevo Presidio de Sn Agustin del
Tuquison, de donde se volverá por los mismos

parages à su Presidio.

Sn Agustin del Tuquison.

157.   La de este Presidio cortará, saliendo por la Mision de Sn Xavier del Wac al Ojito de Agua, trayendo à su derecha la Sierra grande de Santa Rita, y à la izquierda la de Santa Catarina, siguiendo su marcha por las margenes de el Rio de Sn Pedro, parage de Tres Alamos, hasta el Presidio de Sta Cruz, de donde se regresará sobre su propria huella hasta su Presidio.

Presidio de Sta Cruz.

158.   La escuadra de este Presidio cortará, saliendo por el Vado de las Palominas à la Soledad, y de alli por Tierras llanas, y sin sierras, ni domerias que no las ai, y costeando la renombrada Sierra de chiricagui llegará al Presidio de Sn Bernardino, de donde volverá à su Presidio sobre la misma huella que llevó.

Presidio de Sn Bernardino.

159.   La de este Presidio cortará saliendo por la Tinaja, la penosa cañada de Guadalupe, por el Llano de Sn Luis, dexando à su mano derecha la Sierra de Enmedio por la Pelotada hasta el Presidio de

71

Tanos, de donde marchará à su Presidio sobre la misma huella.

Presidio de Tanos.

160.   La escuadra de este Presidio cortará à la Estancia de Becerra, Puerto de los Nopales, y dexando sobre su derecha la Sierra de la Escondida, llegará al Presidio de S.ⁿ Buenaventura, de donde volverá sobre la misma huella à su Presidio.

Presidio de S.ⁿ Buenaventura.

161.   La de este Presidio cortará, saliendo por el Puerto à las Bazas, Ojo de S.ᵗᵒ Domingo, hasta el Presidio de el Carrizal, de donde tomará por los mismos parages la vuelta à su Presidio.

S.ⁿ Fernando de el Carrizal.

162.   La de este Presidio cortará saliendo por la Laguna de Patos al Ojo de Leon, y dexando sobre su mano izquierda la Sierra de la Rancheria llegará al Presidio de S.ⁿ Eleseario, y de aqui se regresará sobre las propria huella à su Presidio.

Presidio de S.ⁿ Eleseario.

163.   La escuadra de este Presidio cortará à los ojos

calientes, Casson chico, y por las orillas de el Rio grande de el Norte seguira su marcha hasta el Presidio de el Principe, desde donde podrà regresarse
para su Presidio.

Presidio del Principe:

164. La de este Presidio deberà cortar por las margenes del Rio grande del Norte hasta el de la Junta de los Rios, desde donde tomarà vuelta para
su Presidio sobre la misma huella.

Presidio de la Junta de los Rios.

165. La de este Presidio cortarà saliendo por los
Puliques al Ojo de Agua de Sn Joseph, al de la
Consolacion, al de Sn Carlos hasta el Presidio de
este nombre, desde donde se regresarà por los
mismos parages al suio.

Presidio de Sn Carlos.

166. La escuadra de este Presidio cortarà al Arroyo
de el Alamo, parage de la Zabaneta, al de las Peñitas, dexando sobre su izquierda la Sierra de
los Chizos, y en llegando al Presidio de Sn Saba
volverà al suio por el mismo rumbo.

Presidio de Sn Saba.

73

167.   da de este Presidio cortará por la valida de el
cañon al Aguage de la Salada, las Torresitas,
las Cruces, ö la Cuesta de los Capitanes, parage de las Cabras hasta llegar al Presidio de san
Antonio Bucareli de la Bavia, volviendo de
aqui al suio sobre la misma huella.

Presidio de S.n Antonio Bucareli.

168.   da de este Presidio cortará à las Rositas de
S.n Juan, la Sierra de el Pino, y cruzando esta
se dirigira por las margenes de el Rio grande
de el Norte, hasta el Presidio de Santa Rosa
en el parage llamado agua verde, reconociendo el paso de Rabayo, y el Bolson que forma
entre el Rio grande de el Norte, y dicha Sierra
de el Pino: y examinando todo este terreno
con la maior proligidad se volverá por los mismos parages à su Presidio.

Presidio de Sánta Rosa.

169.   da escuadra de este Presidio cortará por las
margenes de el Rio grande de el Norte al paso de
Santa Therera, al de S.n Antonio à la Junta de
los Rios grande de el Norte, y S.n Diego, hasta
el Presidio de la Monclava, de donde regresará
sobre la misma huella para el suio.

[74]

Presidio de la Monclova.

170.　La de este Presidio cortará por las margenes de el
Rio grande de el Norte, hasta donde se junta el
Rio Escondido con aquel, y de alli al Presidio de San
Juan Baptista, regresando por el mismo rumbo à
su Presidio.

Presidio de Sn Juan Baptista.

171.　La escuadra de este Presidio cortará cruzando
el Rio grande de el Norte hasta el de las Nueces,
en donde se juntará con la de el Presidio de San
Antonio de Bexar, y dandose los Oficiales mutuamente recibo, se volverá por el proprio camino, à su Presidio.

Presidio de Sn Antonio de Bexar.

172.　La de este Presidio cortará saliendo al parage
de el Atarcoso, al Rio de Medina, hasta llegar
al de las Nueces, en donde deberá juntarse con
la Escuadra de el Presidio de san Juan Bautista, y dandose los oficiales mutuamente recibo de averse encontrado en dicho Rio de las
Nueces, se regresará por los mismos parages à
su Presidio.

Destacamento del Arroyo del Cybolo.

173   La Escuadra de este Destacamento saldrà rumbo al Oriente cortando hasta el parage delas Tetillas, en donde encontrarà la del Presidio dela Bahia del Espiritu Santo; y dandose los Oficiales mutuamente certificacion de averse juntado en dicho parage, marcharà sobre la propria huella à su Destacamento.

Presidio dela Bahia del Espiritu Santo.

174.   La escuadra de este Presidio cortarà saliendo por las Garcitas al Arroyo deel Arrastradero, à las Tetillas, donde se juntarà con la escuadra del Destacamento deel Arroyo deel Cibolo, y dandose los oficiales mutuamente certificacion de aver estado en dicho parage, volverà sobre la misma huella à su Presidio.

175.   Todas, y cada una de las referidas Escuadras deben estar fuera delos Presidios, empleadas en cortar, y revistrar los Terrenos que à cada una se asignan por el tiempo de quince dias.

176.   Corresponderà prevenirles, que por ningun motivo varien de dichos rumbos, ni parages, sino solo en el caso de encontrar alguna huella delos Enemigos que entre, ò salga, la que siendo fresca, ò de poco tiempo deberan seguirla: y si lograren alcanzarles, y reconocidos hallaren no pasar de cien hombres, deberan atacarlos sin alguna detencion, salvo que puedan

conseguirse sorprenderlos à la mañana siguiente.

171. Si el numero delos Barbaros excediere de cien hombres; y dan tiempo por estar arranchados à que se junte con la Escuadra, ò Escuadras delos Presidios immediatos; les dara el aviso correspondiente, supuesto que por el Derrotero asignado à cada Escuadra podra hacerse cargo delas distancias, y parages en que puedan hallarse.

178. Los capitanes deberan alternar en esta tan indispensable, como laudable fatiga con los Thenientes, y Alferezes, de suerte que cada uno salga quince dias con su escuadra. Alas veinte y quatro horas de aver llegado la una, saldra la otra, que hade estar dispuesta, y bastimentada para este fin; de modo que siempre se verifique estar todas en un movimiento continuo.

179. Los Capitanes, y Subalternos formaran, como yà queda dicho un Diario puntual de los acaecimientos mas particulares en sus quince dias, y delas funciones que lograren tener con los enemigos, como serà preciso muchas veces, y en este caso deberan notar el parage; el numero de los muertos, y heridos, si pudiere ser; y delas personas, Cavallos, y Mulas que les tomaren: è igualmente los muertos, y heridos, y otra qualesquiera perdida de nuestra parte:

remitiendolo cada mes los Capitanes à la Comandancia, para que el Jefe principal esté plenamente instruido de quanto ocurriesse
assi favorable, como adverso.

180.   Las Escuadras del Cuerpo Volante de la
Expedicion, pueden ocupar los mismos terrenos,
que se señalan desde el Presidio de Fronteras hasta
el de S.ᵑ Antonio Bucareli dela Bavia haciendo
sus cortadas de el mismo modo que queda prevenido para las Presidiales.

181.   En la Villa de chiguagua siempre se hà mantenido una Compañia para su resguardo, y el de
su circunferencia.

182.   Otra de el proprio Cuerpo Volante està desti-
nada à cubrir todo el Terreno que media desde
el parage llamado Ancon de Carros inclusive
hasta el Presidio viejo de el Gallo, con la mira de
impedir los robos, y muertes que cometen los
Barbaros que se introducen por el Bolson de
Mapimi à las immediaciones del Parral, Valle de S.ᵑ Bartholomè, R.ˡ de el Oro, Hacienda
dla Zarca, y todo aquel rumbo.

183.   Con estas providencias, que son las que Yo
hice observar, no solo se lograra guarnecer la
Frontera, abrazando nuestras Escuadras diariamente las quinientas leguas poco mas, ò meno,
que ai desde el Presidio dela Bahia de el Espiritu
Santo, hasta el de S.ᵗᵃ Gertrudis de el Altar, sino
tambien librarse los moradores de la Vizcaya

de los continuos asaltos que experimentaban.

184.　　　No será menos importante el que por medio de las Escuadras se reconozcan con frecuencia las Sierras que se hallan á espaldas de nuestra linea de Presidios para impedir que en ellas se anochelen los enemigos que suelen introducirse por aquella con tal sutileza, que las escuadras destinadas á cortar los terrenos muchas veces no los sienten, hasta despues que han cometido ya la averia en lo interior de la Provincia.

185.　　　Para que este reconocimiento se haga con la puntualidad, y conocimiento que conviene, nombraré aqui las Sierras, y parages, en que suelen abrigarse los Indios que se introducen por nuestra linea, y son las siguientes: el Pastor de la Mula, el Barrigon, Agua nueva, Sn Antonio, Sn Bernardo, los Reyes, el Venado, las Lagunas, el Alamo Palo blanco, el Nogal, Chilicote, Rancho de Lemus, el Alamillo, Noria de Encinillas, Sta Rosa, Ojo del Buey, Potrero de el Coronel, Victorino, Maxalca, Nieto, Guarachi, Cueva, Torreon, Durazno, la Estacada, Sn Pedro, Chuvizca, Chibato, Vallecillo, los Charcos, el Embudo, el Torreoncillo, la Calera, Mapula, Potrero de la Griega, Mesa de Carretas, Corral de Piedra, Soto, la Silla, Sierrita de Sn Pedro, Cienega de los Padres, el Osito, Potrero de la Dominguez, Rancho de Sierra, Potrero de la Herran, Sierra del Burreon, Chorreras, las

tintas, Hormigas, Escondida, Pastor dela Escon
dida, Coyame, Sierra delos Azados, Potrero
de l'Viñeta, Agua zarca, Cañada de Juan lar
go, Muralla, Cañada dela Mula, Alamillo
de las Cruces, Cañon delos Cerros Colorados,
Azanzazu, Namiquipa, Cañada de el Oso,
Sierra de Sn Phelipe, Picacho de Sierra, Vilchis, Farcate, Metate, Tepehuanes, Quemada,
Rincon, Elvira, Sn Diego, Cañada de Miguel,
Valle de Santa Clara, Sierra de Enmedio, carcay, la Escondida, Cañada de Guadalupe, y
demas que se hallan rumbo al Poniente.

186.　　　　Por el de el Oriente deben reconocerse, y con
Tropa suficiente à quatro Cienegas: y llegando à la parte de el Bolson de Mapimi, que
està immediato à la Provincia de Coahuila,
harà las siguientes maniobras.

187.　　　　Sentarà su Real en el Potrero, de cui-
parage saldrà una Escuadra por la parte deel
Sur à reconocer quanto sea posible las immediaciones de Parras, y aguages que intermedian; haciendo lo mismo por el Poniente à
distancia de veinte, ò veinte y cinco leguas.
Concluido esto se reconoceran los Aguages que
estan immediatos como son el Potrero, Calaveras, Agua verde, y demas, levantando el Real
para acamparse en el Ojo de el Capulin, desde
donde se recorrerà la entrada de Sardinas, y
Boca deel Aura. Acabado esto saldrà una

Escuadra à reconocer por la parte de el Poniente à
distancia de veinte y cinco à treinta leguas, y repre-
sada esta, seguirà la marcha para poner su Real
en el Ojo de el Carrisalexo entrando por el repri-
do rumbo del Poniente de cuio parage saldrà à
batir el intermedio que ai hasta la Tinaja del
Femaute. Hecho esto continuaran su marcha por
el cañon de Zacate de Enfalma, y seguirán dos
Escuadras entrando la una por el Puerto, y la otra
por el cañon, procurando juntarse las referidas
Escuadras en la Hacienda de S.n Joseph, en los
Charcos de S.n Pedro, õ en el Ojo de S.ta Maria,
en la inteligencia que me parece serà mejor en
S.n Joseph, si huviesse Agua bastante, respecto
à que desde este parage està mas proximo para
reconocer el Puerto del Espadin, Aguage de S.n
Eugenio, y salir por el Puerto de Santa Teresa
à la referida Agua de S.ta Maria, y batir el ter_
reno que intermedia desde este Puerto à la Sierra dela Cuesta delos Capitanes, reconociendo los
Aguages de S.n Bartholome, la Salada, y demas
hasta llegar al Paso de S.n Vicente en el Rio
Grande del Norte, desde donde se represará
por los mirmos parages à la Provincia de Coahuila.

188.   Teniendo la Guerra ofensiva por objeto la Paz,
y siendo el de maior atencion el bien, y la conversion delos Yndios Gentiles, y la tranquilidad
delos Paises de Frontera, deberà tenerse siempre

presente, que los medios mas eficaces de conseguir
tan utiles, y piadosos fines son el vigor, y acti-
vidad en la Guerra; y la buena fee, y dulzura
en el trato con los rendidos dados de paz, ó pri-
sioneros.

189. Ambos obgetos podran lograrse en mi
concepto siempre que se tenga por conveniente abrazar á un mismo tiempo todo el terreno que ocupan los perfidos Apaches de Oriente à Poniente, y de Sur à Norte por medio de
diez Destacamentos que se podran disponer
en la forma siguiente.

Destacamentos, ō Divisiones que se pueden formar para la Campaña General.

130. El Destacamento de coahuila que debera ser
el primero, puede componerse de veinte y cinco hombres de cada uno de los Presidios de Sn Juan Baptista del Rio Grande del Norte, Monclova,
Sta Rosa, y Sn Antonio Bucareli; cien Indios
amigos, y cincuenta vecinos: y en todo componen (inclusos los Oficiales subalternos que de
los referidos Presidios, se tubiere por conveniente elegir para el mando de sus respectivas Escuadras) el numero de doscientos setenta y
cinco hombres.

131. El segundo Destacamento podrá componerse de treinta hombres del Presidio de Sn Saba

incluso un Oficial: veinte y cinco de el de S.ⁿ Carlos
veinte y cinco de el de la Junta de los Rios: y
otros tantos de el de el Principe: que en todo componen el numero de ciento y cinco hombres.

192. El tercero Destacamento podrà componer
se de quarenta hombres de el Presidio de San
Elexeario, y cien vecinos, è Indios auxiliares,
que à este fin pueden remitirle de el Pueblo de el
Paso de el Norte: y en todo componen ciento y
quarenta hombres.

193. El quarto Destacamento puede formarse de
doscientos hombres, y cien Indios amigos de las
Milicias de el Pueblo de el Paso de el Rio de el
Norte, que gustosos hacen estas salidas por el
lucro de el pillage: y en todo componen el numero de trecientos hombres efectivos.

194. El quinto, y sexto Destacamentos pueden
componerse en el nuevo Mexico de los Vecinos,
è Indios amigos que se hallan en aquella
Provincia, y que por su situacion no hacen falta
para la defensa de la Frontera de los Indios
Cumanches.

195. El septimo Destacamento puede formarse
de los quarenta y seis hombres de que se compone la Compañia Volante de Sonora, si antes
no se extingue: veinte y cinco de cada uno de
los seis Presidios de su Governacion, y ciento y
cincuenta Indios de la Nacion Opata: que entre
todos componen el numero de trescientos qua-

renta y seis individuos efectivos.

196. El Octavo Destacamento que deberá mandar en persona el Comandante en Jefe, por proporcionarle su situacion de poder comunicar sus ordenes con prontitud á los demas Destacamentos, puede componerse de sesenta Dragones; doscientos y cincuenta hombres, inclusos los Indios Auxiliares de el Cuerpo Volante dela Expedicion: veinte y cinco individuos de cada uno delos Presidios Carrizal, Sn. Buenaventura, y Janos: y en el todo componen el numero de trescientos ochenta y cinco hombres efectivos.

167. El nono Destacamento puede formarse de una dlas Compañías de el Cuerpo Volante dela Expedicion, cuio numero de hombres es el de ciento veinte y cinco, inclusos sus veinte y cinco Indios auxiliares.

198. El decimo, y ultimo Destacamento podrá componerse de cincuenta hombres, inclusos algunos Indios auxiliares.

Derrotero que deberán seguir los Destacamentos nombrados para la Guerra ofensiva, ó Campaña General.

199. El primer Destacamento podrá verificar su salida desde el Presidio de Agua verde en el dia que se asione, dirigiendo su marcha

[84]

por las Bacas, orillas del Rio grande del Norte, hasta donde se junta con este el de S.n Pedro, y desde el nacimiento de este ultimo seguira su derrota al Rio colorado, registrando en su marcha todos los rincones, Sierras, Cañadas, y Aguages que se hallan sobre su derecha, è izquierda, con toda la proligidad, sigilo, y cautela que se requiere para sorprender (si es posible) à los Indios en donde puedan estar arranchados.

200   El segundo Destacamento dispondrà su salida desde el Presidio delas Juntas delos Rios Norte, y Conchos, dirigiendo su marcha al Alamo, la Cienega de S.n Jacinto, el Puerto dela Peña blanca, Tarcate, al Agua delgada, las Adargas, cuio parage se halla en distancia de medio quarto de legua del Rio Colorado, por cuias margenes se dirigira à la Rinconada, ò parage en que se junta este Rio con el grande de el Norte, siendo regular que en este transito se encuentre con el Campo de Coahuila, advirtiendo que en todos los antecedentes se hallan Agua, y Pastos, à mas dela gran ventaja de ser jornadas proporcionadas, y toda Tierra llana.

201.   El tercero Destacamento saldrà desde el Presidio de S.n Elezeario, dirigiendose à la Sierra de Guadalupe, por el Caxon grande, la Tinaja, Carrizo, la Salineta la Grande, Guadalupe, y registrando en su transito la Cola del Aguila, Sierra del Diablo, la del Mogano, y su Cordillera, es-

85

perará en la Sierra de Guadalupe, ō sus immediaciones nueva orden de lo que deba executar.

202.   El quarto Destacamento saldrà por
los Organos, Petaca, reconociendo toda aquella
Cordillera hasta la Sierra blanca, en donde
se juntarà con el Campo dela Nueva Mexico, debiendose hallar en aquella Sierra indis-
pensablemente el dia que se tubiere por conveniente prevenirle.

203.   El quinto Destacamento que debera
salir del nuevo Mexico, dirigirà su marcha
por la Sierra obscura à la Blanca, en donde
se juntarà con el quarto Destacamento, manteniendose ambos en dicho puesto hasta nueva
orden, y con destino se impedir la retirada de
los Indios que puedan huir del Campo, que
va à los Mimbres, y Sierra de Gila, proporcio-
nando el Destacamento sus marchas de tal
modo que se verifique su arribo à la expre-
sada Sierra Blanca el dia que se tubiesse
por conveniente prevenirle.

204.   El sexto Destacamento que deberá tam
bien salir del nuevo Mexico dirigira su
marcha por la espalda dela sierra de los ladrones, registrando la dela Magdalena,
y encaminandose à la de Fr. Christoval de
parte del poniente, se mantendrà en dicho
puesto hasta nueva orden, debiendose verificar
tambien su arribo à èl en el mismo dia que

se huviesse tenido por conveniente prevenir à
los antecedentes Destacamentos quarto, y quinto,
à fin de impedir la retirada por el expresado
puesto de los Yndios que fueren huiendo à los
demas campos.

205.   El septimo Destacamento dirigirà su marcha
por la Sierra de Chiricagui, abrazando al Rio de
Gila, è internandose à la Sierra de este nombre
la continuarà hasta encontrarse con el Rio gran
de de el Norte, en donde se mantendrà hasta el
arribo de el Comandante en Gefe, procurando se
verifique el suio à dho parage el dia que se tubiere por conveniente prevenirlo, si lo permitie-
ren las novedades que pueden ocurrir en su
marcha.

206.   El octavo Destacamento desde el Presidio de S.n
Buenaventura dirigirà su marcha por el Corral de Piedra, la Florida, el Cerrogordo, abrazando la Sangre de Christo, Corral de S.n Agustin à bajar al Muerto en el Rio grande de
el Norte, en donde se juntara con el septimo
Destacamento en el mismo dia que se prefixare,
y despues continuarà su marcha à la Sierra
Blanca, la de el Sacramento, y Guadalupe, no solo
con la mira de adquirir noticias de los progresos
que consiguieren los campos destinados à dichos
parages, sino tambien à dictar sus providencias para la continuacion de la Guerra.

207.   Con la justa mira de que à espaldas de

los Presidios no quede Enemigo alguno, que durante las operaciones de Campaña hostilize lo interior de las Provincias saldrà el nono Destacamento por el Bolson de Mapimi, y reconociendo con toda proligidad sus Sierras, y Aguages, y particularmente las de Acatita la grande, y la de Baxan, continuarà su marcha à la Sierra dela Paila, è immediaciones de Parras, y al regresarse por la Provincia de Coahuila à la Villa de Chiguagua, reconocerà el Carrizalexo, la Tinaja de el Fernauxe, por el Cañon de Zacate de Enoalma, Ojo de Sta Maria, Puerto del Espadin, Aguage de S.n Eugenio, y saliendo por el Puerto de Sto Thereza al Aguage de S.ta Maria, batirà el terreno q.e intermedia desde este Puerto à la Cuesta de los Capitanes, reconociendo el Aguage dela Salada, y demas hasta el Paso de S.n Vicente, y de aqui tomarà por el Presidio de S.n Carlos, la Mula, Potrero dela Herran, hasta la Villa de Chiguagua, à cuio Comandante debe dar cuenta de los progresos conseguidos en la Expedicion de su cargo.

208. El decimo, y ultimo Destacamento saldrà dela Villa de Chiguagua dirigiendose à la Sierra de Santa Clara, Valle de este nombre, y de aqui continuarà su marcha, reconociendo todas las Sierras que ai hasta el Rio de Temehuaque: y despues de aver dado cuenta

al Capitan del Presidio de Janos, delas novedades que aian ocurrido en su expedicion, darà vuelta à la propria Villa, esperando nueva
orden delo que debe executar.

203.   Todos, y cada uno delos referidos Destacamentos deberan hallarse en los terrenos que
à cada uno se asigna en los dias que se les prefixare, y por ningun motivo variaran de los
rumbos citados, sino solo en el caso de encontrar alguna huella de los Enemigos, que deberan
seguir siendo fresca, ò de poco tiempo, y si lograren alcanzarles, y reconocidos hallaren
no ser superiores en fuerzas deberan atacarlos sin alguna detencion, salvo que se pueda
conseguir sorprenderlos al siguiente dia.

210.   Si el numero delos Barbaros fuere exce-
sivo, y con estremo ventajoso el terreno que
ocuparen, y dieren tiempo por estar arranchados, à que se junte con el Destacamento, ò Destacamentos immediatos les darà el aviso correspondiente, supuesto que por el Derrotero asignado à cada Destacamento, podrà hacerse
cargo delas distancias, y parages en que puedan
hallarse.

211.   Los Comandantes delos Destacamentos deberan formar un Diario puntual delos acaecimientos mas particulares en su Expedicion,
y delas funciones que lograren tener con los
Enemigos, y en este caso individualizaran el

parage, y demas circunstancias, esmerandose
mui particularmente en el cuidado delas Presas que hicieren, hasta que se les proporcione
ocasion depoderlas remitir al Presidio mas
immediato: Cuios Documentos dirigiràn al
Comandante en Gefe, para que por ellos venga
en conocimiento delas operaciones de cada
uno, y sean consiguientes sus providencias.

212.   Respecto à que por el Derrotero pueden los Comandantes graduar el tiempo qe.
estaran en Campaña, deberan disponer los
Bastimentos correspondientes, proporcionan-
dolos de tal modo, que no llegue el caso de
faltarle al Soldado la racion diaria, que con
arreglo à Ordenanza debe subministrarsele:
y para su cumplimiento se pasaran las Ordenes
correspondientes à los respectivos Habilitados
en tiempo oportuno.

213.   Los citados Comandantes no omitiran diligencia alguna conducente al logro de los apre-
ciables fines, à que se dirige una fatiga tan
util: pues de este modo se reconoceran mas
individualmente los terrenos de los enemigos;
podrà seguirseles muchas veces sin dilacion;
seràn precisos los encuentros, y choques con
las Escuadras, o Partidas de ellos; advertiran
la vigilancia, y constancia con que nuestra
Tropa se mantiene sobre su terreno; no en-
traran en el nuestro con libertad; hallaran

en el rigor de nuestras Armas el justo castigo q.e
merecen: resultando de todo la tranquilidad de
las Fronteras.

244.   Para el mando de estos Destacamentos podran elegirse entre los Capitanes de la Frontera
aquellos mas activos, è instruidos en los terrenos
de que se trata; maximas, y astucias de los Enemigos; y parages en que suelen emboscarse,
de conocido valor, è inteligencia en el modo de
hacer la Guerra à los Indios, prefixandoles el
dia en que todos los Destacamentos deben verificar su salida à Campaña, que será sin duda
en uno mismo desde los Presidios, y parages
que quedan indicados.

Campañas particulares.

245.   Ademas de la Campaña General podran pra-
ticarse otras particulares contra los Apaches
de el Poniente que habitan las Sierras de Chiricagui, Gila, y la de los Mimbres, de donde los
rechazan los immoderados frios de los meses de
Diciembre, Enero, y Febrero, obligandoles por
consiguiente à buscar su Asilo en otras de mas
moderado temperamento.

216   El castigo de estos podrà lograrse comple-
tamente, disponiendo la salida en los meses de
Febrero, ò Marzo, desde el Presidio de Janos
de tres Escuadras competentes en la fra. sig.te

247. La primera Escuadra debe dirigir su marcha por el Rio abaxo à las Viznagas, parage llamado la Espia, la Boca de Guzman, Carrizal, Saucitos, y el Aleman, en donde esperarà el arribo de la segunda, y tercera.

218. La segunda Escuadra deberà salir en el mismo dia que lo aia practicado la primera, siguiendo su marcha por la Palotada, à la Sierra de Enmedio, S.n Luis, por el Peñol de d.n Gabriel, à caer al Aleman, en donde se juntarà con la antecedente.

219. La tercera debe hacer su salida à los tres dias que aian practicado la suia la primera, y segunda, siguiendo su marcha por la punta de el Mal-Pais à la Palotada, Ojo de el Perro, Ojo de Beitia à caer por la orilla de la Sierra de la Hacha al Aleman en donde se juntarà con las otras.

220. Vnidas yà las tres Escuadras reconoceràn con prolixidad, y el maior silencio que sea posible para no ser sentidos por los Enemigos antes de tiempo, la Sierra de la Hacha, en donde, como en los demas parages indicados, hallaran seguramente à los Enemigos, ocupados en la fabrica de el Mexcal, que hace mucha parte de su sustento. Proveidos de el que necesitan para su gasto se retiran con sus familias à la Sierra de los Mimbres à mediados de el mes de Abril para sembrar

sus Maices, Frixol, y Calabaza en las cañadas dela misma Sierra, cuia ocasión parece igualmente oportuna para el castigo, y podrá lograrse por medio de un Destacamento, compuesto quando menos de ciento y cincuenta hombres mandado por un Oficial instruido en aquellos terrenos.

224.   El hacer fuego con conocimiento; cargar con brevedad; guardar formación; romperla, y reunirse para sostenerse, guardando el oportuno silencio, deben considerarse las maniobras suficientes para la calidad de Enemigos con que se exercita esta Tropa, y sus individuos se hallan bien instruidos en ellas.

222.   Siempre que se tenga por conveniente aumentar en la Frontera alguna Tropa, por el conocimiento practico que me asiste, Juzgo lo mas aproposito al efecto, los que se recluten, y den plaza en aquellas Tierras, por ser estos los que con menos dificultad se acomodan á la extraordinaria fatiga de esta Guerra, en todo diversa á la dela demas gente politica, respecto à no poderse observar otra disciplina, principalmente para ofender à los Indios, que lo misma suia.

223.   Consiste esta en ser hombres diestros à cavallo: saber disparar una Escopeta: manejar la Adarga, que es como natural en ellos: correr con aguante muchas leguas de dia, y de noche: sufrir Sol, Sereno, Agua, y Nieves; sin otro alim.to

93

à veces, que un poco de Maís molido deshecho en agua, que llaman Pinole; ni mas Tienda de abrigo, que la que ofrece un Capote: y de este modo se podrá suplir la falta de los Fusileros de Cataluña, que pedi al Govierno con fecha de 8. de Marzo de 74.

221.   En la guerra que se haga contra los Apaches, siempre opinaré como conveniente, que se emplee à los fidelissimos Indios Opatas, assi por su acreditado valor, como por su gran conocimiento delos Terrenos, Sierras, y Aguages en que habitan los Indios Apaches de el Poniente. Ellos se aprontaran para las salidas que se hagan en el numero, y tiempos que el Comandante determinare, pues jamas huvo exemplar de que faltassen al cumplimiento de quantas ordenes seles comunicaban, manifestando en todas ocasiones el constante amor que professan à los Españoles: cuios hechos con su aplicacion à la Agricultura; afan con que procuran enseñar la Doctrina Christiana à sus hijos, y su particular esmero en el Culto Divino, les hace en mi concepto acreedores à que sean atendidos, y mirados con amor, distinguiendolos delas demas Naciones.

225.   Detalladas ya todas las disposiciones que reputo conducentes à la guerra defensiva, y ofensiva contra Apaches; resta solo exponer el concepto que hago de los Indios conpre-

gados en Pueblos, y Misiones con distincion de Provincias, sin olvidar el perjuicio que algunas de
ellos hacen en lo interior de aquellas.

226.   En la de Sonora ai à mas dela Nacion
Opata los Indios Seris, los Pimas altos, y baxos,
los Tiburones, y los Yaquis. Las Seris, y Pimas
altos se congregaron de resultas dla Expedicion Militar de Sonora en los Pueblos de el
Pitic, Pitiqui, Caborca, Visanic, Sn Antonio de
Oquitoa, el Ati, Sta Thereza, Tubutama, Saric,
Sn Xavier del Wac, y Sn Agustin deel Tuquison, y à todos los vi quando estube en la Provin
cia con muestras à miparecer de mantenerse
quietos, y fieles, y aplicados los mas de ellos à
la Agricultura, excepto unas veinte familias qe.
desertaron el Terreno, y à quienes se han atri-
buidos algunos daños acaecidos, y delos Tiburones ninguno se refiere mucho tiempo hace, segun
los informes dlos Tejs dla Provincia, que existen
en el Archivo de Chiguagua.

227.   Mucho mas quieta, y util la Nacion Yaqui se emplea de continuo en el Rl dla Cienequilla,
y otros Minerales dla Sonora, à que son afectissi-
mos. Los Pimas baxos viven tranquilamente en
sus Pueblos immediatos al Presidio de Sn Miguel
Orcasitas con suma aplicacion al beneficio de
sus Labores, y al comercio que con los Españoles
tienen.

228.   En la Provincia de Nueva Vizcaya viven en

diversos Pueblos las bastas crecidas Naciones de
la Tarahumara Alta, y Baxa, y estos à título
de Apaches son los que cometen muchos daños
en lo interior de ella; pero estos excesos, sino me
engaño provienen de el ningun arreglo en las
Poblaciones, y en la vexacion con que se les trata:
pues estando prevenido por Ley, que los mandamientos que libren sean para la tercia parte
de los Indios de cada una, se cometen excesos
grandes; de modo que ai vez que ninguno queda
en el Pueblo para atender à la familia de los
ausentes.

229.   Siguese à este tirano perjuicio la mala paga de los Hacenderos, y el peor modo con que
se les trata, y como por su aussencia en los tiempos precisos de siembras, y Cosechas, les llega
à faltar el mantenimiento; veen à sus familias
en cueros, y muertas de hambre, no es estraño
que resueltos à buscar auxilios, cometan robos, y otros daños para sufragar la necesidad,
cayendo en el herror de muchos homicidios
para no ser descubiertos.

230.   El superior Govierno hà librado repetidas
providencias para el arreglo de estos Pueblos
con la justa mira de precaver tales excesos: y
esto nunca podrà lograrse à menos que el
Justicia de cada uno no indague todos los dias
el paradero de sus Indios; y se proceda para
contenerlos en quietud en los Mandamientos

que se libran, conforme à las Leyes; cuio asunto
le tengo por dela maior atencion, y preferencia,
como que sin resolverle, siempre sucederan
daños en la Provincia, y sin saberse con realidad quien los cometa, aunque por lo comun
se atribuyen al Apache.

231.   En la Provincia de Coahuila ai varios Pueblos de Indios, pero solo los Tulimeños han dado
hasta ahora motivo de recelo por su constante
amistad con los Apaches. Es necesario que se vele
mucho sobre su conducta para saber si son ellos
los actores de muchos robos, y otros excesos que
seles imputan, pero para vivir sin tal cuidado,
siempre opinarè convenir seles haga regresar
à su antiguo Pueblo de Tulimes en Nueva Vizcaya, baxo del de una Persona fiel, que pueda
zelar sus movimientos, y dar cuenta oportunam.te

232.   En la Provincia de el Nuevo Mexico,
que se halla mas de un grado fuera de nuestra
Linea ai los Indios Temes, Silla, Sta Anna, Sandia, la Isleta, Pueblo de Genizaros, Laguna, Acu-
ma, los Navajoes, y otros que no conozco, pero
see que todos se dedican pacificamente entre
si à la Agricultura de sus Tierras, y à la Cria
de Ganados maiores, y menores, de que disfru-
ta en tal abundancia que raro año ai en que
no pasan de dos mil Cabezas las que remiten
de venta à los Presidios dela Linea, sin otros efectos como Medias, Frezadas, y Texidos, acre-

ditando assi su laboriosa aplicacion.

133.   Cerca de el Pueblo de el Paso de el Norte ai otros quatro de Indios, conocidos por los nombres de Pios, Mansos, Sumas, y Piguas que viven con la maior sugecion à los Ministros Doctrineros, y à la Justicia ordinaria aplicados à sus Labranzas, y en especial al cultivo delas Villas, de que abundan aquellos Terrenos: y aunque todos son proprios para la Guerra por su experimentado valor, y conocimiento delas Sierras, y Aguages que por aquellos rumbos habitan los Apaches, nunca produciran favorables efectos las salidas que hacen contra ellos voluntariamente por la falta que les infiere el Destacamento Stablecido prevenido en la Nueva R.¹ Instruccion, cuio establecimiento suspendieron hasta ahora los Informes que hizo el Brigadier d.ⁿ Pedro Fermin de Mendinueta.

134.   La delos Texas q. se halla tambien mas de un grado fuera de nuestra Linea ha sido de las ultramarinas de España la mas costosa, aunque poco util; la mas estendida, aunque ignorada; y la que mas hostilidades ha producido; pero la que mas importa por muchos titulos, como que ninguna delas otras puede entrar à su paralelo. Linda por el Oriente con la de la Luisiana, ò nueva Orleans: por el Poniente con el Rio de Medina: por el Septentrion con el Misuris: y por el Medio dia con el Mar, ò

Seno Mexicano: tiene caudalosos Rios que la
riegan; Serranias que la rodean, y defienden; Valles, y Llanuras que piden de Justicia manos la-
bradoras; y se puebla de una numerosa Genti-
lidad, que atrahida al reconocimiento, y Vasallage deel Monarcha la haria mas fertil, y rica
que las otras Provincias por su situacion, Sentio,
y bello Clima.

235.   Los Indios que viven en ella al abrigo de
nuestros Presidios, y pasan por amigos son: Texas, Orcoquisac, Vidaes, Asinais, Navedachos,
Nasonis, Yatasis, y Caudachos, todos de un
proprio Idioma. Ay tambien los Tehuacanes,
Yxcanis, y Taobayas, que aunque parecen tres
Tribus, hacen un Pueblo, si bien separado en
otras tantas parcialidades: y estos son à quienes
principalmente se culpa delas irrupciones co-
metidas años pasados contra el Presidio de
Sn. Saba, y no falta quien apoye aver sido pro-
bocados à ellas con opresiones, y otros malos
tratos.

236.   Aunque ellos no sean verdaderos amigos
nuestros, lo son ciertamente delas otras Naciones; se aman reciprocamente, y demas de la
union que les resulta por causa de sus Cam-
balaches, ay otra razon politica en ellos, que
nunca permitira la separacion de sus intereses, y convendria atraer por buenos medios las
citadas tres Rancherias para que fuessen

amigos, respecto à que cierran el paso à los in-
quietos Indios Guazas, y otros belicosos de el
Norte, que confinan con las posesiones Inglesas,
cuia codiciosa Nacion nada apetece mas q.^e
internarse por aquellas partes.

237.   Al Poniente delos Tuacanes, Yxcanis,
y Taovayas estàn los Cumanches nativos, y
dueños de el dilatado Pais, que encierran las
Cordilleras de el Nuevo Mexico, y el caudaloso
Rio Misuris: gentio tan crecido, y sobervio, que
ellos proprios se ponderan con el numero de las
Estrellas: son diestros en el manejo de el cavallo,
y Lanza, y de mucho tino en disparar flechas:
viven siempre baxo de Tiendas, vagando de
un lugar à otro, sin hacer mas mansion q.^e
la que necesitan, hasta que con la Caza se
proveen de Ciervos, y Cibolos de que sacan
su alimento, y Vestuario.

238.   La precision en que antes se veian para
solicitar uno, y otro de pasar por las immediaciones delos Tuacanes, Yxcanis, y Taovayas
era causa de que los Cumanches no hiciessen
en ellas mas que una mansion momentanea,
è inquieto, por que miraban estas Naciones,
como Dominio de un Enemigo poderoso, de
quien siempre recibian fatales golpes, por
el alcance de el Fusil; pero confederados despues todos, libres de su aprehencion, y con
iguales Armas, se estiende ya tumultuosam.^te

desde lo mas remoto deel Norte hasta el Pais
mas meridional, pareciendo vengarse assi de
aquel impedimento que avian tanto tiempo
hace esperimentado.

239.   Tambien los Apaches que cortaban al
Cumanche el paso, por hallarse en el camino
son (aunque opuestos unos con otros,) enemigos cada uno de nuestras Provincias de Texas,
y Nuevo Mexico, donde han cometido san-
grientos insultos, y entre todas las Naciones referidas es el mas temible, assi por las
Armas de fuego adquiridas de Yngleses, q.
sabe manejan diestramente, como por su
valor, è intrepidez, y por que nunca acos-
tumbra huir, prefiriendo antes el morir,
ò vencer: de lo que, y de el modo que tienen
de hacer la guerra, hà dado en estos ultimos tiempos muchas pruebas de ser mal
civil, y politico, que los demas Barbaros
sus colindantes.

240   A la parte de el Medio dia, ò por mejor
decir en la costa de el Seno Mexicano, con-
tigua al Presidio dela Bahia de el Espiritu Santo vive arranchada la Nacion
Carancaguax, que si bien hasta à hora cau-
só poco cuidado, se hà visto estos ultimos
dias lo perjudicial que es su vecindad para los que naufragan en ella, contra quienes
han exercido muchas inumanidades: oy

parece tenerlos amigos, ò en una especie de
subordinacion el Capitan d.n Luis Cazorla;
pero como quiera que ellos se mantienen
infieles, y sirven de abrigo à los Apostatas
de aquellas Misiones; me parece conveniente seles persuadiera à la reduccion, ò se les
forzara, como que son pocos, à vivir con
los demas Neofitos; por que no pudiendo
ser utiles en los naufragios de Embarca-
ciones, que con frecuencia dan al trevèz en
aquella Costa; vale mas que los que se
salvan la hallen desierta, que no el que
caigan en sus manos à experimentar sa-
crificio: escusandose assi la ereccion deun
Fuerte modernamente consultado, à que
opuse mi dictamen, segun puede verse por
los Documentos de el Archivo de Chiguagua.

241.　　　Si su establecimiento tubiera por
obgeto el que se propuso d.n Luis Cazorla
seria ciertamente util à los Navegantes
en los peligros de que aquella Costa abunda;
pero acaso con el se abriria mas el paso
al Comercio ilicito, de que no necesita
mucho la Provincia delos Texas, atendida
la posesion en que està de el por muchas
partes con la proximidad de Ingleses, y
Franceses, cuia razon es la misma que
tube, y tendrè siempre para opinar en
contra dela Poblacion de N. S. deel Pilar

de Bucareli en el sitio en q.^e se halla, por q.^e como situada en el centro delas Naciones infieles referidas, recibe por conducto de todas quantos efectos consume la Provincia, y otros q.^e se internan en las immediatas con quienes colinda, sin q.^e hasta àhora aian bastado providencias à la correccion de tales daños.

242.   Me hè detenido en la descripcion de esta Provincia, y sus habitantes mucho mas q.^e en la delas otras por menos conocida, y por que siendo el unico Valuarte q.^e esta Nueva España tiene, contra las dos Potencias de Inglaterra, y Francia, hè creido justo indicarlo por si con mis apuntes, y las demas noticias q.^e adquiera V.S. determinare aplicar sus conatos à hacerla feliz, reduciendo tantos Indios, como pueden atraerse al Vasallage, en cuio caso poco podrà temerse delos vecinos, pues la dilatada esten, cion q.^e habitan seria su maior embarazo.

243.   Creo con lo expuesto aver correspondido bastantem.^{te} al deseo de V.S. assi por q.^e sepa el estado en q.^e Yo hallè las Fronteras, quando recibi el mando de ellas, como lo obrado en todos sus terrenos, y constitucion en que las dexè.

244.   La diferencia q.^e se nota de un tiempo à otro solo hà podido conseguirse à costa de un quantioso desembolso del Erario; del Zelo mio; y de fatiga en la Tropa. Esta tiene oy una superioridad invencible sobre los Barbaros. Pocos de estos se atrevian antes à triplicado numero delos nuestros; y yà sucede todo

al contrario, por los repetidos golpes q.e han recibido.

245.   Sin embargo nunca faltaran en las Fronteras rapiñas, robos, muertes, y otras hostilidades, por no ser facil impedir à los Indios en el todo la entrada q.e astutam.te suelen hacer algunos Peloteros sin ser sentidos por las Esquadras; pero bien dispuestas las Cortadas, y ocupados con Destacam.tos los parages mas sospechosos, podrà remediarse mucho, tenerlos refrenados, y en quietud aquellos Vecindarios, y Poblaciones, con interes deel Herario, y Publico.

246.   El Plan q.e propongo en este papel es el q.e me enseñaron mis experiencias; el q.e hice observar; y el q.e fue feliz à mis tales quales progresos; por malo q.e sea no dexarà de dar à V.S. luces de mucha conveniencia, è importancia al Servicio; pero no teniendo Yo empeño alguno en q.e se siga, ni menos en q.e sirvan de Norte otras disposiciones que alumbro, queda al arbitrio de V.S. tomar para sus aciertos lo que juzgue ventajoso, y asequible = N.S. q.e à V.S. muchos años. Mexico 22 de Julio de 1777 = B.L.M. de V.S. su mas atento seguro Servidor = D.n Hugo Oconor = Señor D.n Theodoro de Croix.

104

106

107

110

DATE DUE

Printed
in USA

HIGHSMITH #45230